PEOPLE ECONOMICS

Defining and Measuring the True Value of Human Capital

Laura Kellers Queen

ISBN: 978-1-09839-095-2 (print)
ISBN: 978-1-09839-096-9 (eBook)

Table of Contents

APPENDICES

Preface

IT'S EXCITING TO LIVE IN A TIME WHEN WE ARE FINALLY seeing a new awareness of how to measure business success. After decades of thoughtful discussion and recommendations, investors, business leaders, economists and policymakers are finally taking concrete steps to include people in the measures of what does and does not make a successful company. To date, we have used an incomplete calculus, and I am inspired to share the new world that is taking shape.

To be honest, for those of us who are U.S.-based, that change has been significantly slower than in many other countries. Our country, despite being formed on the powerful words "We the People …," has not stepped up to the leadership plate to define and measure the true value of human capital. My decision to write this book was driven by a need to synthesize the many conversations about human capital measurement and to demonstrate that we *can* find and apply meaningful and understandable metrics to measure the worth of employees in financial terms, especially when making decisions relating to acquisition, valuation and investment.

Because my career has spanned both the financial and human resources spectrum, I have a unique perspective of where systems in organizations break down and fail to communicate with each other. The result is often stagnation, the failure of workers to thrive and even the demise of companies. My global experience with businesses large and small has allowed me to see the real-life daily impact of decision-making in a way that is not always crystal-clear to academics, investors and policymakers. As a dedicated life-long learner, I have also been on a constant road to discovery, talking with experts across disciplines from around the world.

I have chosen the title and term *People Economics* because that's what we are talking about: putting people front and center in the development and application of economic models. Like any terminology, it has flaws, and I truly wanted to get the big picture out there — that economics is not about numbers but rather, how those numbers create a sustainable and equitable life for people who make things, provide services, share their creativity and affect our lives every day.

I hope this book will bring some clarity and different perspectives to both decision-makers in companies and investors. I hope it will help frame new ways of thinking for students pursuing degrees in business, human resources and economics so they bring fresh, evidence-based ideas to the table. I hope anyone who is concerned about how work and social values interact will find these ideas stimulating.

Since my intention is to inspire dialogue, I have tried writing this book at a level that will be understandable for people who are not currently involved in the issues of human capital. To that end, I spend time early in the book on defining both highly used and new terms, as well as talking about the players in this new approach to economics. Defining the language sets a common baseline for discussion. Do feel free to refine and add other terms as well as players. Nobody has been left out intentionally.

Let me tell you a bit about how the book is organized.

In the first section, I make a case for People Economics and define the issues and history. The second section offers perspectives from experts whom I believe bring interesting ideas to the table. Section Three provides real stories from my consulting experience. Finally, I have added an appendix that includes calculations that marry two of the most-important standards in the field. The other appendix shows examples of how companies are currently disclosing information in ways that have never been done before.

While this book is of interest to traditional publishers, I have chosen to self-publish because of timing. (It can take almost two years from accepted proposal to distribution for a book to reach the market with traditional publishing.) The world of human capital is changing so rapidly, and I did not want information to be obsolete before it hit my readers' libraries. I also want it to have an impact on the current debate.

I am looking forward to a dialogue with those reading my book. Please send your thoughts and ideas to me at laura.queen@29bison.com and lend your voice to the conversation via social media on Twitter and Instagram @peopleecon.

Acknowledgments

I OWE MOUNTAINS OF GRATITUDE TO THE MANY PEOPLE AND organizations who have inspired this exploration. I might overlook people in this list and for that you have my most sincere apologies; know your contribution lives in my heart and on these pages. For your deft hand, candor and amazing support, Kathy Palokoff (goFirestarter), my book coach. To Dave Bookbinder for inspiring this conversation, allowing serendipity to be a guide and your constant friendship. To Katie Desiderio for your enthusiasm, joy and magic — we are dreaming a bigger dream, together. To my companions and other direct contributors to this book Doug Claffey, John Dumay, Karen Fenner, David Griffith, Rick Joi, Sarah Kim, J. Renay Loper, Aeisha Mastagni and Amit Mohindra. You have each contributed more than you can imagine and enriched this work beyond measure.

To the many generous souls who have opened their emails, phone lines and Zoom meetings to me, leading me down this path; among you are Mary Adams (IIRC), Amy Armitage (HC IRC), Sonya Aronowitz (Juniper Agency), Jeff Cohen (SASB), Jennifer Fondrevay (Day1Ready), Stathis Gould (IFAC), Jeff Higgins (HCMI), Denise Logan (Chase What Matters), Bob Nolan (Halyard Capital) and Kelli Okuji-Wilson (SASB). For your partnership and creativity before the world was ready: Mare Rosenbaum. To all the leaders of businesses and organizations who have committed your efforts and lent your voices to sustainable organizations, positive work environments and inclusive capitalism — this work is built upon the foundations you have laid. My humble hope is it will advance your cause.

To Jason A. Wood for "not hating the idea," believing that nothing is impossible and then actually making it possible. To Kevin Dougherty for lending your ear and your skills with stickie notes. To all our children and their partners, our friends, and family members for being by my side as I embarked on yet another expedition. To Tim, the love of my life, for allowing me space and providing tireless support and encouragement as I follow my passions. Finally, to Otis and Izzy for your unconditional love and affection, constant companionship and warmth — both literal and figurative.

THE CASE FOR
PEOPLE ECONOMICS

CHAPTER 1

The Human Cost

THE PHONE RANG AT 9:30 P.M. ON A BITTER TUESDAY EVENING in late January, and I could hardly understand Dottie as she sobbed. Shaking my head in sadness and bewilderment, I listened for a few minutes, handed the phone to my husband and headed up the stairs to tuck our toddler into bed. Now I stood cold and numb in a graveside chapel. Laid out before us was a shattered life, so beautiful and vibrant only weeks before. I was alone since Bob, my husband, had been summoned by his new employer to a mandatory meeting, so I represented our family, heartbroken and disillusioned, with tears streaming down my face.

Here is how it all began. The previous Friday, Bob and the team he managed at our local bank was told their department was being eliminated, as the result of an acquisition by a large regional bank. Dottie was a member of his team. While my husband was offered a new role with the bank, everybody else lost their jobs. Bob and I were relieved that he still had a job because with a large mortgage and small child we needed the security, yet we felt terrible about the impact on his colleagues since many were personal friends and neighbors. At the time, I was the site administrator for a government-funded county agency charged with helping dislocated workers retrain and search for new jobs. Many of the bank employees affected by these job eliminations would be coming to me for career transition services.

These were people we knew intimately; we attended church together and had been to each other's weddings, baby showers and birthday parties. One of them was our daughter's godfather. Making matters even more difficult was that my husband's team was angry, confused and resentful because he and I still had good jobs. We struggled with survivors' guilt and the fear of losing long-time personal relationships, which were so important to us. We were all trying to come to grips with a new reality and the various personal and professional consequences of this business transaction.

A week before we heard the news about the bank, Dottie's husband, Steve, also lost his job. A 25-year employee of a global telecom company, he took tremendous pride in his work. His position allowed him to serve his local community and create a loving, stable home for his family. Much of how he described himself was borne of the job he did; it defined him and gave him personal meaning and significance. His identity was stripped away with the stroke of a pen as yet another business restructured. The news that Dottie was also losing her role, after nearly 20 years with the bank, left Steve overwrought and overwhelmed. He was paralyzed and convinced he could no longer provide for his wife and two teenagers. Unable to see a clear path forward, Steve lost his sense of self. On that bleak Tuesday evening in January, Steve sought solace in the outdoors. Asking for some time to gather his thoughts after dinner, he went for a walk and behind their garden shed, took his life with a shotgun.

Now, in the thin gray morning light of the graveside chapel at Steve's funeral, my worldview shifted and I swore an oath. My purpose in life would be to rewrite stories like Dottie and Steve's. I would put people front-and-center, making them the subject of my life and not the object of my work. That moment is etched into the core of my being and will always inform what I do and why I do it. It has become my calling and guidepost, and I have shared this story with friends, family and colleagues over the years.

Needless to say, I am not infallible and have made missteps along the way, some with gut-wrenching consequences to others. Every day, I seek to be forgiven for those hurtful decisions and to be rewarded with the opportunity to start again new with a fresh perspective. One thing I deeply believe: The requirement to consider the human lives we touch in every act and particularly our businesses should be of paramount concern to us all. Business decisions are a fact of life; evolution and transitions are what offers the opportunity for personal and professional growth and renewal. Yet alongside these expected ebbs and flows, we must remember there are enormous implications for our actions. As leaders, we have the power to influence the lives of our employees, co-workers, constituents, community members, neighbors, friends and family members inordinately, in obvious and not-so-obvious ways. We have an obligation, as fellow humans, to wield this power wisely and responsibly.

In his book *The Road to Character*, David Brooks speaks of being "obedient to our calling" in service by finding depth of character.

> *... We don't create our lives; we are summoned by life. The important answers are not found inside, they are found outside. This perspective begins not within the autonomous self, but with the concrete circumstances in which you happen to be embedded. This perspective begins with an awareness that the world existed long before you and will last long after you, and that in the brief span of your life you have been thrown by fate, by history, by chance, by evolution or by God into a specific place with specific problems and needs. Your job is to figure certain things out: What does this environment need in order to be made whole? What is it that needs repair? What tasks are lying around waiting to be performed? As the novelist Frederick Buechner put it, 'At what points do my talents and deep gladness meet the world's deep need?'*[1]

I carry Dottie and Steve's story in my heart. As to my own story, I emerged from Moravian College as an undergraduate with a degree in industrial and organizational psychology and a deep passion for how people and business intersect. A lifetime learner in formal and informal settings, I've continued this exploration unabated. In fact, had the field of behavioral economics existed when I was an undergrad, I would have leapt in headfirst. The works of Daniel Kahneman, Amos Tversky, Richard Thaler, Dan Ariely and Nassim Taleb are frequent visitors to my iBook's library and bedside table.

After an early career in finance and administrative positions, I shifted into human resources for local, regional and global companies. My roles have included responsibility for human resources in all its various shapes and sizes; occupational health and wellness; environmental health and safety; physical security; loss prevention and cybersecurity; DEA diversion control; and aviation. Over the course of my career, I have personally laid off or terminated thousands of people. I have participated in dozens of mergers, acquisitions, joint ventures, restructurings and divestitures, valued at more than $50 billion in transactions and counting. In each and every case, I have struggled with knowing the impact and implications of the decisions, delivery of the messages, and ripple effects I may never personally witness. I have told every one of my staff members over the years that when I can sleep soundly the night before I have to let someone go, it is time for me to toss in the towel.

My career also led me to Tim, my second husband, soulmate and love of my life, and graced us with three amazing children and their families. It has provided me with a trove of friends and colleagues, including my business partners, colleagues and alliance partners, many of whom count as my extended family. It has allowed me to pursue a joy of learning and with new, forever friends, including a former FBI hostage negotiator and professor at the Navy War College; a U.S. Army General; a host of elite defense contractors and cybersecurity specialists; and a strategy executive for Exxon/Mobil. It has blessed me with thousands of LinkedIn connections from places all over the world in all kinds of roles with varied interests and perspectives.

Over time, I have come to adore the cities of San Francisco, Vina del Mar (Chile), London and Tel Aviv, and cultivated a love for the wines and food of the Middle East. My travels have allowed me to amass a treasured photographic collection of street art from Santiago and Valparaiso, Munich, Salzburg, Oahu, the 9th Ward of New Orleans, Tribeca (New York), Cambridge and Boston, Philadelphia, and many, many other places.

As David Brooks and Arianna Huffington remind us, no one will be reading our resumes from the lectern at our funerals. Eventually, there came a point in my career when I needed to find a way to help differently, to make a larger difference. My professional partners and I believe there is an imperative to revolutionize the way we handle business transitions, and it begins with putting people at the center of the process rather than as an afterthought. Our experience tells us success lies in finding a means to account for and educate others about the value of human capital in organizations. The magic elixir is a common language shared by all stakeholders so we can change this imbalanced calculus. Together we can propel decision-makers to an accounting and economic worldview that embraces a "both, and" perspective — organizations and their people can be *both* successful *and* thrive through an investment in people.

In his 2018 letter to the CEOs of the organization in which Blackstone invests, Larry Fink said: "… society increasingly is turning to the private sector and asking that companies respond to broader societal challenges. Indeed, the public expectations of your company have never been greater. Society is demanding that companies, both public and private, serve a social purpose. To prosper over time, every company must not only deliver financial performance, but also show how it makes a positive contribution to society. Companies must benefit all of their stakeholders, including shareholders, employees, customers and the communities in which they operate."[2]

I believe we are on the cusp of a deep and meaningful change. As my dear friend Dave Bookbinder, an accomplished author and corporate valuation specialist, says: "The value of business is a function of how well the financial capital and the intellectual capital are managed by the human capital. You'd better get the human capital part right!"[3]

A HISTORICAL PERSPECTIVE

Too often we forget to frame new ideas in a historical context. To quote Maya Angelou, "If you don't know where you've come from, you don't know where you're going." Let's take a few moments for a brief history lesson relating to people and economics.

In 1776, Scottish philosopher Adam Smith, commonly regarded as the father of modern capitalism, wrote *An Inquiry into the Nature and Causes of the Wealth of Nations.*[4] Considered the seminal work of modern economic theory, it lays the foundation for a free-market economy and basis for libertarianism. His perspectives are often misconstrued and misinterpreted as the siren's call for the accumulation of riches as the sole purpose of economic endeavor.

In a similar vein, 2020 marked the 50th anniversary of Milton Friedman's famous essay, "The Social Responsibility of Business is to Increase its Profits," where he wrote, "There is one and only one social responsibility of business — to use its resources and engage in activities designed to increase its profits so long as it stays within the rules of the game, which is to say, engages in open and free competition without deception fraud."[5] The winner of the Nobel Prize in economics argued that a corporate executive "… has direct responsibility to his employers. That responsibility is to conduct the business in accordance with their desires, which generally will be to make as much money as possible while conforming to their basic rules of the society, both those embodied in law and those embodied in ethical custom."

According to Friedman, executives of organizations such as hospitals or schools are the exception, allowing that providing a specific service, rather than profit-making, is their primary objective. In all cases, the role of the executive is as an agent to his employers, the owners and shareholders. To act in social interests is the purview of civil servants who are to be elected and relegated to being a part of the "political machinery." He does, however, leave room for business leaders to do good and support social aims at their own expense.

Long before Milton Friedman, enterprises — especially manufacturers — sought avenues to ensure the highest levels of profits through human performance and productivity. The United States' Industrial Age dawned at the turn of the 20th century and ushered in unprecedented opportunities for commercial expansion, growth opportunity and solidifying America as an industrial and economic powerhouse. This era led to standardization of work processes, optimizing workflows, simplifying jobs and incenting worker cooperation. These efforts were largely built on *The Principles of Scientific Management*[6] devised by Frederick W. Taylor, concepts often referred to as Taylorism. His views were based in part on the erroneous assumption that all workers were motivated by money. Businesses flourished after adopting Taylor's premises; a prime example is Ford Motor Company and the proliferation of assembly line production.

An unintended consequence of these mechanisms for higher levels of production was the dehumanization of employees. Tragic consequences ensued. Upton Sinclair's *The Jungle*[7] offers a glimpse into the ghastly world of meatpacking during the early 1900s. It was a relatively common occurrence for workers to be maimed or mortally wounded at work. There was no compensation to them or their families for loss of life or limb. In the absence of the injured worker, a foreman would walk out to the gate and choose another able-bodied worker to take his place.

Similarly, under the assumption that seamstresses would abandon their duties if left to their own devices, 146 mainly female employees died in New York City's Triangle Shirtwaist Fire in 1911 because exit doors were locked and chained to keep them at their machines. It took 59 years from that fire for President Nixon to sign the Occupational Health and Safety

Act (OSHA) into law and create the Occupational Safety and Health Administration.

At the same time Milton Friedman's essay was being lauded by contemporary capitalists, Klaus Schwab formed what we now know as the World Economic Forum, where he continues to serve as executive chair. In 1973, he produced the first "Davos Manifesto: A Code of Ethics for Business Leaders." It declared: *"The purpose of professional management is to serve clients, shareholders, workers and employees, as well as societies, and to harmonize the different interests of the stakeholders."*[8] The principles harken back to Adam Smith's first set of observations and principles in 1759 in his book, *The Theory of Moral Sentiments*, in which he beautifully articulated the requirement for empathy and consideration of people, and the failure of human cognition to adopt the perspective of others: "Though our brother is upon the rack, as long as we ourselves are at ease, our senses will never inform us of what he suffers. They never did and never can carry us beyond our own persons, and it is by the imagination only that we form any conception of what are his sensations ... His agonies, when they are thus brought home to ourselves, when we have thus adopted and made them our own, begin at last to affect us, and we then tremble and shudder at the thought of what he feels."[9]

As a nation and a society, we believe we have matured into more-responsible and -caring work environments. The truth of that matter is health and safety issues have only shifted. Job loss and material insecurity, especially for those who lose jobs before retirement age, cause higher risks for suicide and overdoses compared to active employees. Toxic work environments, characterized by high levels of workplace- and project-related stress, lead to a range of physical and mental health problems. Workers in these environments may suffer from diseases such as depression, anxiety and insomnia, all of which contribute to low employee morale and negatively affect productivity.

During the COVID-19 pandemic, we witnessed our fragility. The lack of physical safety for front-line healthcare workers, schoolteachers, grocery store clerks, sanitation workers, restaurant employees and delivery drivers has affected individuals, families and communities. The fear of contracting a deadly virus, absence of necessary protective equipment, physical fatigue, mental exhaustion and emotional overload brought us directly back to the turn-of-the-20th century. In the midst of the pandemic, we were also forced to reckon with a 9 minute and 29 second reminder of how far we have yet to go: "I can't breathe, I can't breathe, Somebody HELP ME, I can't breathe!" Images of George Floyd and the aftermath of his death showed us we are a nation at war with itself.

From the dawn of our country to the present, we have struggled with issues of harassment, discrimination and racism. Civil war, riots, looting, politics, art, science, music, culture, personal relationships, the definition of marriage and families have been informed by inequality. We suffer a propensity to objectify people, seeing "them" as other than ourselves, rather than as whole beings who deserve respect, dignity and compassion. As in every generation before us, there is a crucible moment offering us the gift of an opportunity to see ourselves with fresh eyes. May 25, 2020 — fittingly Memorial Day — was our day.

Throughout the history of the United States, it has been primarily white men who have benefited from systems designed to limit opportunity for people of color, women and immigrants. We are facing a new actor on this stage as we begin to see issues of social caste and employment discrimination wind their way in our courts. The state of California filed a suit against Cisco, for instance, alleging discrimination and retaliation in employment on the basis of social caste. In October 2020, the suit filed on behalf of a Dalit (Indian) engineer was voluntarily dismissed by California's Department of Fair Employment and Housing.

WORDS ARE IMPORTANT

One of the most important things I have realized as we sought to put people at the center of economics and not as an afterthought is that words are very, very important. Accounting and financial practices are not just about numbers. They are about the words and phrases that define the meaning behind the numbers. These terms come from history and are often loaded with the biases and beliefs of the world at that time. I have sought out the words being used today to reflect the critical new approaches we need to do business. I have also created a few terms, which may help create a common and approachable language about the concepts I describe in this book.

One term is the title of this book, *People Economics*. I will discuss this in-depth; for now what I mean is an economic system placing people first in all areas of business including in valuation, investment and operations. The study of value creation through the dynamic interactions of an organization's intangible assets and environment through the lens of human capital is People Economics. Another term I will use is PeopleAlpha. PeopleAlpha are the ways in which operating with a focus on people enhances investment outcomes, adds financial value in investments, and contributes to stronger and more productive workplaces.

Please note the use of the word "people" in both of these terms.[10] At the end of the day, our financial systems exist to provide people with quality of life. It is just that simple and why I have included chapters in this book that share stories of the real people who are affected by economic decisions.

United, we are a new generation of leaders and influencers. We have the power to make a difference; to change the paradigm; to embrace a holistic view of the concept of value; to craft more human and humane work experiences; and to provide benefit and improved outcomes of all kinds for every stakeholder. We have the power to change the story for people like Dottie and Steve.

CHAPTER 2

The Players

IT'S A CONFUSING WORLD OUT THERE. THAT STATEMENT IS true for both newbies and experienced followers of business. It's a world filled with acronyms and jargon, so I want to make sure that you understand some of the key players in human capital standards and measurement, as well as both traditional and new language being used in businesses and economics.

This chapter will quickly provide an overview of the organizations you need to know about in a brief listing of influencers of the dialogue about human capital. The list is not inclusive and is constantly changing. In the following chapter, I will lay out definitions of the changing language of People Economics.

CAPITALS COALITION

In 2018, the World Business Council for Sustainable Development (WBCSD) formed The Social & Human Capital Coalition to bring together "those who specialize in measuring the value that people and society create for one another." In 2019, the Social & Human Capital Coalition joined forces with its sister organization, the Natural Capital Coalition, "to ensure that the value of nature and people sits alongside financial value in the minds of decision makers at all levels." Renamed the Capitals Coalition, the organization primarily focuses on private organizations and seeks to "change the system by reflecting the true value of nature, people and society in all decisions." Their three-pronged approach to change addresses business and financial measures of nature, people and society — change the math; motivations and incentives driving decision-making — change the rules; and communication and growing supportive communities — change the conversation.

The Capitals Coalition defines capital as "a resource or asset that stores and provides value to people. When invested in and managed responsibly the asset creates value. If we 'draw down' on the capital stock itself we limit its ability to provide value to people and the economy, and if we degrade it too much, it can stop providing value all together." Like the International Integrated Reporting Council (IIRC), the Capitals Coalition advocates an "integrated thinking" approach. Similar to many of the other available capital frameworks introduced in this chapter, the Capitals Coalition recognizes and defines natural capital, social capital, human capital and produced (manufactured) capital; however, the model does not recognize intellectual capital as a separate component of their framework. However, in their January 2021 Principles of Integrated Capitals Assessments,[11] the Capitals Coalition suggests reporting organizations may prefer to use the International Integrated Reporting Council's six capitals definitions (which you will be introduced to shortly) for greater granularity in their reporting.

COALITION FOR INCLUSIVE CAPITALISM

The Coalition for Inclusive Capitalism is a global not-for-profit organization established to engage leaders among business, government and civil society in their efforts to make capitalism more equitable, sustainable and inclusive. The Coalition develops practical thought leadership and convenes the Conference on Inclusive Capitalism to bring together renowned leaders from the world's largest and most-influential asset owners, asset managers and corporations to positively influence the future of capitalism.

ESG CENTER AT THE CONFERENCE BOARD

The ESG Center provides insights in the areas of corporate governance, sustainability and citizenship in the areas of environment and social governance — commonly referred to as ESG.

FINANCIAL ACCOUNTING STANDARDS BOARD

The Financial Accounting Standards Board (FASB) is a private, non-profit organization standard-setting body whose primary purpose is to establish and improve Generally Accepted Accounting Principles within the United States in the public's interest.

GLOBAL REPORTING INITIATIVE

The Global Reporting Initiative (GRI) is an international, independent standards organization that helps businesses, governments and other organizations understand and communicate their impacts on issues such as climate change, human rights and corruption.

GOVERNMENT ACCOUNTING STANDARDS BOARD

The Governmental Accounting Standards Board (GASB) is a private, non-governmental organization (NGO) that is the source of generally accepted accounting principles (GAAP) used by state and local governments in the United States.

HUMAN CAPITAL MANAGEMENT COALITION

The Human Capital Management Coalition (HCMC) is a cooperative effort among a diverse group of influential institutional investors to further elevate human capital management as a critical component in company performance.

INTERNATIONAL ACCOUNTING STANDARDS BOARD

The International Accounting Standards Board (IASB) is an independent, private-sector body that develops and approves the International Financial Reporting Standards (IFRS).

INTERNATIONAL BUSINESS COUNCIL

The International Business Council (IBC) is a global organization committed to advancing global economies by fostering business and leadership development opportunities among governments and businesses worldwide by delivering highly specialized and integrated concepts of high-level summits, meetings, digital collaboration, publications, professional development programs, market intelligence and expertise. The IBC is a unit of the World Economic Forum.

INTERNATIONAL INTEGRATED REPORTING COUNCIL

The International Integrated Reporting Council (IIRC) is a global coalition of regulators, investors, companies, standard-setters, the accounting profession, academia and NGOs. The coalition promotes communication about value creation as the next step in the evolution of corporate reporting. In November 2020, the IIRC and the Sustainability Accounting Standards Board issued a joint statement regarding their intention to merge, and formed the Value Reporting Foundation.[12]

JUST CAPITAL

Seeking to restore trust in capitalism, JUST Capital's research, rankings, indexes and data-driven tools help measure and improve corporate performance in the stakeholder economy.

OCCUPATIONAL SAFETY AND HEALTH ADMINISTRATION

The United States Congress created the Occupational Safety and Health Administration (OSHA) to ensure safe and healthful working conditions for working people by setting and enforcing standards and providing training, outreach, education and assistance.

ORGANISATION FOR ECONOMIC COOPERATION AND DEVELOPMENT

The Organisation for Economic Cooperation and Development (OECD) is an intergovernmental economic organization with 37 member countries, founded in 1961 to stimulate economic progress and world trade.

SUSTAINABILITY ACCOUNTING STANDARDS BOARD

The mission of the Sustainability Accounting Standards Board (SASB) is to help businesses around the world identify, manage and report on the sustainability topics that matter most to their investors. SASB standards are developed based on extensive feedback from companies, investors and other market participants as part of a transparent, publicly documented process. SASB standards differ by industry, enabling investors and companies to compare performance from company to company within an industry. SASB and the IIRC announced their intention to merge, forming the Value Reporting Foundation in November 2020.

UNITED STATES DEPARTMENT OF LABOR

The United States Department of Labor (DoL) is a cabinet-level department of the U.S. federal government responsible for occupational safety, wage and hour standards, unemployment insurance benefits, reemployment services, and some economic statistics.

UNITED STATES SECURITIES AND EXCHANGE COMMISSION

The U.S. Securities and Exchange Commission (SEC) is a large, independent agency of the United States federal government created after the stock market crash in the 1920s to protect investors and the national banking system.

WORLD BUSINESS COUNCIL FOR SUSTAINABLE DEVELOPMENT

The World Business Council for Sustainable Development (WBCSD) was established in 1995 as a platform for business to respond to sustainability challenges that were just beginning to break the surface of collective business consciousness. Comprising more than 200 leading organizations and more than 19 million employees worldwide, the WBCSD represents more than $8.5 trillion USD in annual revenue. It is a CEO-led organization and connected to 60 national and regional business councils and partner organizations. Similar to the other organizations in this book, the WBCSD aligns its mission with the United Nations Sustainability and Development Goals (UN SDGs).

WORLD ECONOMIC FORUM

The World Economic Forum (WEF) is the international organization for public-private cooperation. The Forum engages the foremost political, business, cultural and other leaders of society to shape global, regional and industry agendas.

CHAPTER 3

The Changing Language of Business

"We must always reject the false choice between making a profit and making a difference. When you deliver a positive impact on people, the planet, and the communities you serve, you create the conditions for both business and society to thrive."

— ENRIQUE LORES, PRESIDENT & CEO, HP INC.

THE LANGUAGE OF BUSINESS IS IN FLUX, STRONGLY LINKED to a rapidly changing society and the ways that stakeholders measure success. COVID-19, social unrest, racial injustice and the emergence of a multi-stakeholder view of the economy are tilling up fertile soil in which to plant the seeds of a new era. Our times have highlighted the importance of people to businesses, economies and the fabric of our communities. Issues of physical safety, mental health, financial and economic uncertainties loom larger than we could have ever imagined. It has also shed light on our fragility in an age when being resilient isn't enough. "COVID is not a game changer, it is an accelerator. The world will switch from material success to well-being as indicators of happiness," says Klaus Schwab, founder and chair of the WEF.[13]

Before I build out the concept of People Economics and its implications, implementation and measurement, it is important to begin from the same point with a common language of both traditional and new terms, as well as some important concepts. As much as possible, I have tried to use definitions and descriptive frameworks that non-economists can

understand. Other terms are used throughout the book, and these definitions are important to give you a solid grounding and reference for other
chapters.

ALPHA

Alpha measures the amount an investment returns in excess of its benchmark and is expressed as a percentage. The benchmark may be a market
index, the expected internal rate of return or some other broad measurement. For example, an alpha of 2 for a specific investment project indicates
a return 2% higher than expected against a predetermined benchmark.
Identifying and attributing these excess returns to specific inputs and activities has become increasingly important to business owners and investors
because they can then be used as levers to improve investment outcomes
such as profitability and shareholder return.

CAPITALS

Capital has many different meanings. For this book, I am adopting the
definitions of capital outlined in the Integrated Reporting Framework
(IRF) provided by the IIRC in 2021.[14] The framework outlines six capitals,
three of which are defined here: financial, manufactured and natural.

Financial capital is the pool of funds available to an organization for
use in the production of goods or the provision of service and is obtained
through financing such as debt, equity or grants, as well as generated
through operations or investments.

Manufactured capital refers to manufactured physical objects (as
distinct from natural physical objects) available to an organization for use
in the production of goods and the provision of services, including build-
ings; equipment; and infrastructure such as roads, ports, bridges, and waste
and treatment plants. Manufactured capital is often created by other organizations, and includes assets manufactured by an organization for sale
when they are retained for their own use.

Natural capital includes all renewable and non-renewable environmental resources and processes that provide goods or services to support the past, current or future prosperity of an organization. It includes air, water, land, minerals and forests, as well as biodiversity and eco-system health.

The other three capitals — intellectual, human, and social and relationship — are the subjects of this book and will be defined and discussed in much greater detail in the section about Intangibles, later in this chapter. Remember that capitals are not fixed; there is a constant change in capital as they are transformed through organizational activities. As you will see, there are also competing frameworks and definitions as capital relates to intangible assets or intellectual capital.

EMPLOYEES

It is important to clarify who is an employee. One of the disclosure metrics included in the WEF/IBC framework[15] is adapted from the UK Government guidance on gender and ethnicity pay gap reporting.[16] For the sake of clarity, I have adapted their definition of an employee: Employees are people who are considered regular employees of your organization, whether full- or part-time; workers and agency workers (co-employees, temporary and contingent workers, interns, seasonal employees); and some self-employed people if they are independent contractors receiving a U.S. 1099 or ex-U.S. equivalent workers, but who are not assigned to work for your organization under a supplier or professional services contract (e.g., outside auditors, onsite recruiters under an RPO contract, technology developers being paid directly by the contract organization, etc.).

Further, a full-time-employee (FTE), based on the GRI definition, is an employee whose working hours per week, month or year are defined according to national legislation and practice regarding working time (such as national legislation that defines "full-time" as a minimum of nine months per year and a minimum of 30 hours per week). Consequently, a part-time employee (PTE) is an employee whose working hours per week, month or year are less than full-time.[17]

ENVIRONMENTAL, SOCIAL AND GOVERNANCE

ESG is often used in the context of financial and corporate reporting. We are most-familiar with the "E" component as it relates to environmental issues of climate change, natural resource availability and depletion, and measuring our carbon footprint. The "S" component has gained prominence recently as issues of racial injustice, pay parity and the value of people in business are appearing in all international headlines; labor practices, product safety, employee health and wellness, talent management, and data and information security all live in this category. The "G" component, relating to issues of governance, has gained in prominence over the past few years and includes matters like executive pay and perks, business ethics, and board diversity.

Members of the Coalition for Inclusive Capitalism have begun advocating for a change in the term ESG. They argue it is insufficient to account for workers under the social or "S" category and that employees should be identified as a separate component in this taxonomy. They argue for use of the acronym EESG: Employee, Environmental, Social and Governance.

For proof of how organizations are taking this new language to heart, just glance at these 2020 statistics from JUST Capital, an organization that describes itself as "the only independent nonprofit that tracks, analyzes and engages with large corporations and their investors on how they perform on the public's priorities." Based on their analysis, the companies they tracked had "56% higher total shareholder returns over the past five years; used 123% more green energy; had a 7.2% higher return on equity; emitted 86% fewer tons of PM 2.5 emissions into the atmosphere; paid 18% more to their median workers; were six times more likely to have set diversity targets; were 4.7 times more likely to have conducted a gender or race/ethnicity pay equity analysis; and gave six times more to charitable causes than their peers."[18]

Topics relating to ESG are tied to the United Nations Sustainable Development Goals (SDGs), adopted in 2015. All member states of the United Nations (UN) agreed to a "shared blueprint for peace and prosperity for all people and the planet." The 17 overarching SDGs[19] provide a roadmap for a better world by 2030. Each goal also consists of sub-goals, with the hope that individuals, businesses, communities and member states will each be able to connect with one or more of these goals and adopt them as operating principles tied to the mission, vision and purpose of their efforts and organizations. Any business, small or large, can use these guidelines; my partners and I developed our own company's strategy and corporate impact goals aligned with the UN SDG goals and sub-goals linked to our organization's mission and purpose of "Appreciating [Human] Capital."

Here is a listing of the SDG goals and definitions.

1. No Poverty. End poverty in all its forms everywhere.

2. Zero Hunger. End hunger, achieve food security and improve nutrition.

3. Good Health and Well-Being. Ensure healthy lives and promote well-being for all at all ages, and promote sustainable agriculture.

4. Quality Education. Ensure inclusive and equitable quality education and promote lifelong learning opportunities for all.

5. Gender Equality. Achieve gender equality and empower all women and girls.

6. Clean Water and Sanitation. Ensure availability and sustainable management of water and sanitation for all.

7. Affordable and Clean Energy. Ensure access to affordable, reliable, sustainable and modern energy for all.

8. Decent Work and Economic Growth. Promote sustained, inclusive and sustainable economic growth, full and productive employment, and decent work for all.

9. Industry, Innovation and Infrastructure. Build resilient infrastructure, promote inclusive and sustainable industrialization, and foster innovation.

10. Reduced Inequalities. Reduce inequality within and among countries.

11. Sustainable Cities and Communities. Make cities and human settlements inclusive, safe, resilient and sustainable.

12. Responsible Consumption and Production. Ensure sustainable consumption and production patterns.

13. Climate Action. Take urgent action to combat climate change and its impacts.

14. Life Below Water. Conserve and sustainably use the oceans, seas and marine resources for sustainable development.

15. Life on Land. Protect, restore and promote sustainable use of terrestrial ecosystems, sustainably manage forests, combat desertification, and halt and reverse land degradation and halt biodiversity loss.

16. Peace, Justice and Strong Institutions. Promote peaceful and inclusive societies for sustainable development, provide access to

justice for all and build effective, accountable and inclusive institutions at all levels.

17. Partnerships for Goals. Strengthen the means of implementation and revitalize the global partnership for sustainable development.

The goals and sub-goals that directly tie sustainability to the principles of People Economics and integrated reporting include the following.

SDG GOAL 5: GENDER EQUALITY — INCLUDES THE FOLLOWING SUB-GOALS:

5.1   End all forms of discrimination against women and girls everywhere.

5.5   Ensure women's full and effective participation and equal opportunities for leadership at all levels of decision-making in political, economic and public life.

5.B   Enhance the use of enabling technology, in particular information and communications technology, to promote the empowerment of women.

SDG GOAL 8: DECENT WORK AND ECONOMIC GROWTH

8.2   Achieve higher levels of economic productivity through diversification, technological upgrading and innovation, including through a focus on high-value-added and labor-intensive sectors.

8.3   Promote development-oriented policies that support productive activities, decent job creation, entrepreneurship, creativity and innovation, and encourage the formalization and growth of micro, small and mid-sized enterprises, including through access to financial services.

8.5   By 2030, achieve full and productive employment and decent
       work for all women and men, including for young people and
       persons with disabilities, and equal pay for equal value.

SDG GOAL 16: PEACE, JUSTICE AND STRONG INSTITUTIONS

16.6   Develop effective, accountable and transparent institutions at all
       levels.

16.10 Ensure public access to information and protect fundamental
       freedoms, in accordance with national legislation and interna-
       tional agreements.

16.B   Promote and enforce non-discriminatory laws and policies for
       sustainable development.

GENERALLY ACCEPTED ACCOUNTING PRINCIPLES

Issued by the FASB, GAAP is a standardized set of accounting principles
used in the United Stated by all publicly traded and many private organizations. GAAP is commonly regarded as a "rules-based" system of accounting. Accounting standards outside the United States are generally governed
by the IFRS issued by the IASB through directives called International
Accounting Standards (IASs).

HUMAN CAPITAL

Human capital yields economic value for an organization via the production of goods, services and ideas, through the knowledge, competence,
technical skill, experience, capacity for learning and innovation, and commitment level of an organization's human beings, and the approach to how
they are led and managed. Human capital contributes deeply to an organization's distinctive character and competitive advantage. Let's be very clear:
Human Capital is not human resources (HR), and those who recognize the
difference can leverage a toolkit for growth they never knew existed.

These perceptions have led to the development of a field called Human Capital Management (HCM). Some argue that HCM is merely a grandiose title adopted by HR professionals. This idea stems from the fact that many business leaders are simply unaware that a systematic and quantifiable process exists that can inform critical decisions about people. To clarify, HR covers a wider constellation of organizational activities, ranging from recruitment and onboarding to payroll and benefits administration, and HCM represents a far more-specialized field within HR. It is not unlike the role of a data scientist within the broader IT function. In recognizing the value of employees as a true asset, HCM professionals are tasked with optimizing the business value of the workforce through measurable initiatives, tied directly to company growth.

As you will see, human capital is also one of the six capitals included in the <IR> Framework and one of a handful of capitals referred to as intangibles.

INTANGIBLES

The <IR> Framework includes three capitals: intellectual, human, and social and relationship capital — that are all subcomponents of an accounting concept known as intangible assets or intangibles. Surrounding these terms is a rigorous, ongoing debate and important set of economic and accounting principles.

By definition, an intangible is something that cannot be seen or touched. An intangible asset for accounting purposes is hard to describe or assign a specific value to. It is something that may not have a physical nature yet still has value. The IFRS International Accounting Standard 38 (IAS 38)[20] considers an intangible an identifiable non-monetary asset without physical substance. Intangibles may have tremendous value and won't appear on a company's balance sheet because acquiring intangibles is considered an expense, rather than an investment.

Intangibles include: brand equity, company reputation, goodwill, copyrights, trademarks, patents, intellectual property, customer lists, domain names, employment contracts, lease agreements, client relationships, trade secrets, films, licenses, computer software and codes, permits, import quotas, franchise agreements, cross-marketing agreements, and channel partnerships. Like all intangibles, human capital cannot be expressed on an accounting statement as a financial measure and is considered an expense.

One useful perspective on intangible capital comes from economist, Marco Montemari:

> Over the years, several taxonomies have been proposed to classify IC. A broad consensus was gradually reached on the categorisation that splits IC into human capital, organisational capital, and relational capital. Human capital entails the individual knowledge, competences, skills, and experience of people working within a company. Organisational (structural) capital is the codified knowledge which is structured in "tangible" elements so that it can be shared and transmitted in time and space. It includes databases, information systems, intellectual properties, technologies, software, internal procedures. Relational capital is the network of relationships established with stakeholders, investors, suppliers and, above all, with current and potential customers. It also includes corporate image, reputation, and brand.[21]

Intangible assets (IAs) represent the combination of intellectual capital (IC), human capital (HC) and social and relationship capital (SRC). None of the IA components alone are sufficient for successful value creation and business performance. Rather, value creation is a phenomenon built upon by dynamic interactions, transformations and complementarities arising from activities, processes, rules and relationships. As discussed by economist Daniel Andriessen, "It is always a combination of intangible assets that make a company unique and successful. It is the synergy between intangibles that creates uniqueness and wealth, not the individual assets."[22] Leif Edvinsson, a Swedish organizational theorist, adds to that perspective: "Intangible value is the possession of knowledge, applied experience, organizational technology, customer relationships and professional skills that provides a competitive edge in the market."[23]

The common thread connecting intangibles is that they are created, in large measure, through the efforts of people. On its surface, it may appear helpful to separate intangible assets into independent parts, but that approach is overly reductionist and potentially harmful to a full and complete understanding of value creation and erosion. Because the dynamic interaction between and among these inputs is so valuable and fundamentally derives from the efforts, ingenuity, creativity and nurturing of people, we must pay greater attention to human capital.

In 2019, the IFRS Foundation held a working group. A report of the proceedings leaves us to wonder whether the IFRS Foundation members tasked with establishing international financial reporting standards are connected to the imperatives of the larger investment community who are increasingly attentive to the value of intangible assets, particularly human capital.

"Overwhelming evidence suggests that companies today derive significantly greater value from intangibles than was the case, say 20–30 years ago. We examined a few intangibles — human capital, brands and knowledge. Some approaches measure and value these intangibles — but few participants suggested they be recognized in financial statements. Investors on the panel commented that such recognitions would have little analytical value. In our discussion of these intangibles: a majority, 75% of participants reported that measuring human capital would be of limited use to investors; and just 45% of participants said that knowledge should not *be reported in a company's financial statements. Of the workshop participants, 65% agreed that an*

absence of harmony in current requirements was the greatest obstacle hinder-
ing progress towards the global adoption of intangibles reporting
frameworks."[24]

Substantial efforts to define and measure intangibles in meaningful, quantitative and qualitative ways persist. These efforts are evident in the <IR> Framework's definitions of intellectual capital, human capital, and social and relationship capital, and their integrated thinking construct.[25]

Intellectual capital incorporates organizational, knowledge-based intangibles, including intellectual property such as patents, copyrights, software, rights and licenses, as well as organizational capital such as tacit knowledge, systems, procedures and protocols.

Human capital involves people's competencies, capabilities and experience, and their motivations to innovate, including their alignment with and support for an organization's governance framework, risk management approach, and ethical values; ability to understand, develop and implement an organization's strategy; and loyalties and motivations for improving processes, goods and services, including their ability to lead, manage and collaborate. Human capital yields economic value for an organization through the production of goods, services and ideas; knowledge, competence, technical skill, experience, capacity for learning and innovation; and commitment level of an organization's human beings and the approach to how they are led and managed. Human capital represents an organization's distinctive character and competitive advantage.

Social and relationship capital is the institutions and the relationships within and between communities, groups of stakeholders and other networks, and the ability to share information to enhance individual and collective well-being. Social and relationship capital includes shared norms and common values and behaviors; key stakeholder relationships; the trust and willingness to engage that an organization has developed and strives to build with and protect external stakeholders; the intangibles associated with the brand and reputation an organization has developed; and an organization's social license to operate.

This working model depicts inputs in the form of the various capitals that make up a business. Through the application of business processes, activities, governance, organizational structure and environmental conditions, outcomes produced have a measurable impact on value and transformation of the capitals. Capitals are not fixed; there is a constant change in capital as they are transformed through organizational activities. Transformation of the capitals is an organization's secret sauce and is not easily replicated. As John Dumay, professor of accounting at Macquarie University, advises: "Leaders and investors should strive to better understand the possible causal relationships between their people, processes and stakeholders (human, structural and relational capital) rather than adopting someone else's mousetrap."[26]

It is helpful to think of the six capitals and their relationship to value creation, preservation and erosion using a visual model, such as this one from the <IR> Framework:

Figure 2. Process through which value is created, preserved or eroded

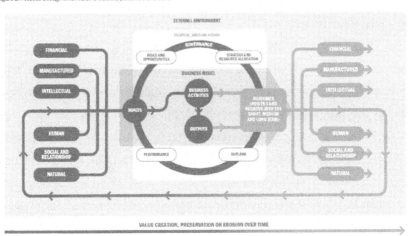

INTERNAL RATE OF RETURN

Internal Rate of Return (IRR) is a measure of potential profitability that is often used by investors to determine whether to pursue an investment project. Generally expressed as a percentage, the IRR shows whether an investment is worth making, based on whether the projected returns are greater than the initial costs.

INTERNATIONAL FINANCIAL REPORTING STANDARDS

The IAS are used in more than 110 countries around the world including Europe. Produced by the IASB, these financial reporting standards are considered a "principles-based" system, whereas the United States GAAP standards are viewed as a "rules-based" system of accounting. There is a growing movement of financial professionals and regulators in the U.S. and around the world who advocate for the adoption of the IFRS standards to better align principles, definitions and reporting across the globe.

INVESTORS

Put simply, investors are sources of funding for a business. Imagine you are an entrepreneur with a patent and a great initial idea for a business. Before you make your first appearance on "Shark Tank," you need proof of concept and this takes money, which is known as funding. You are likely to be your own first investor, draining a savings account, cashing in a bond, selling your family heirlooms or working a second job to support your new idea. As you progress, the first types of outside investors you may seek may be friends, family and close personal contacts. At this stage, you will also look for funding from banks and, perhaps, government agencies. These funds will come in the form of lines of credit (LOCs), credit cards, grants and small business loans. Lenders and government agencies aren't investors per se; however, if they have contributed to your capital, they have a vested interest in the success of your business.

As your business gains traction, you will look for additional sources of investment, more-flexible lending terms, sources of advice and industry connections. Angel investors, angel groups, incubators and accelerators can be helpful. These groups generally invest in what are called seed rounds: very early stages of a business, sometimes even the pre-revenue phases of an enterprise. These investors are willing to make riskier investments than other potential investors and are looking for you to make lightning-fast progress.

Growing your company may require multiple phases of funding, commonly called capital raises. These phases will draw on various potential sources of financial capital to pay back the seed-round investors and provide a platform for continued expansion. Family offices are one such source of capital. These are privately held companies that handle wealth and investment management for a family or a group of very wealthy families; the company's financial capital is composed of the families' financial assets. One aspect of the family office responsibility is to find investment opportunities for direct investments in startups or growth-phase businesses. Family offices are often extremely private and have very specific, family-directed investment goals and interests.

Another possible source of funding at this stage is venture capital (VC). VC is a form of private equity financing made up of funds from third-party investors (individuals and institutions) who take an equity stake in your business in exchange for their financing. It is provided to early-stage, high-growth businesses deemed too risky for standard lenders or investors. Recipients of venture capital often benefit directly from the operations, managerial and technical expertise of their lenders.

Private equity (PE) financing is very similar to VC funding. The primary difference between VC and PE investment strategy has to do with the level of risk and stage of maturity of the businesses each invests in. Private equity looks for larger, more-established businesses with a proven track record of success. Each PE firm has a specific investment strategy, which includes the market segment, size of investment, intended length of time they will invest for (hold period), and the minimum and maximum investments they are willing to make. PE-backed businesses often benefit from both financial and non-financial investments during the hold period.

Large corporations can be friends and allies to early- and growth-stage entrepreneurs. Whether as direct investors or through sponsored incubator and accelerator programs, corporate investors look for opportunities to fuel revenues and profits, infuse talent and technology, and defend against industry changes.

It is important to distinguish institutional investors from individual investors and limited partners (LPs) from general partners (GPs). An institutional investor is an organization that invests on behalf of the organization's members. VC and PE funds, banks, labor union pension funds, insurance companies, mutual funds, and hedge funds are all institutional investors. Individual investors make purchases and trade individual stocks independently through a broker and as an employee participating in a company-sponsored retirement plan. Both individual and institutional investors can purchase individual equities (stock), mutual fund shares, and municipal bonds, and make direct investments in small businesses. However, not all individuals may invest as members of VC or PE firms.

An institutional investor may, and frequently does, make investments in other institutional investment opportunities. For example, as part of a strategic investment strategy a labor union may invest a portion of its assets in the stock market (equities), a portion in municipal bonds, a portion in interest-bearing bank accounts, and smaller portions in venture capital and PE funds. The labor union is then considered an LP in the VC and PE funds. In exchange for their investment, they will receive limited profits from the businesses the VC or PE funds invest in, and their liabilities are restricted to the extent of their investment. In this scenario, the VC and PE funds are considered the GPs. GPs are part owners of the businesses they invest in and may be held personally or individually liable for the debts of the business.

MATERIALITY

Materiality lies at the heart of sustainability and stakeholder capitalism. At its core, materiality seeks to tie items and issues of significance to qualitative and quantitative measures and metrics, which can be used by various stakeholders to determine their importance to stakeholder decision-making. Specifically, this principle is aimed at helping investors understand what is financially important (or *material*) to an organization.

An example of materiality may make this easier to understand. Imagine you and your neighbor both own businesses and you are both trying to determine materiality. You each have automobiles owned or leased by the business. You happen to be in consulting and, other than the occasional lunch or business development meeting, largely operate your business either remotely or from your office. Your neighbor, however, owns a floral shop and is required to pick up flowers from regional distributors, deliver flowers to customers and maintain office landscapes for clients.

In this example, an investor or other stakeholder is likely to conclude that automobile leases, purchases and maintenance are material for your neighbor's flower shop — without them, products wouldn't make it to his customers, which would result in lost revenue for the business. In contrast, they would be likely to view your car lease as an immaterial expense.

PEOPLE ALPHA

People Alpha is the excess returns available to owners and investors through recognizing employees as true business assets and applying a systematic approach to human capital management. People Alpha can be used as a measurement tool before investments to evaluate people-related risks and opportunities. During ownership, People Alpha can be used to optimize the value of the workforce tied to distinct business outcomes, thereby enhancing portfolio company performance and fund-level returns.

STAKEHOLDER CAPITALISM

Stakeholder capitalism, increasingly called inclusive capitalism, refers to a system where corporations serve the interests of all stakeholders with the purpose of creating long-term value as opposed to maximizing the profits of only some stakeholder groups such as investors. That is often referred to as shareholder capitalism.

SUSTAINABLE DEVELOPMENT GOALS

The Sustainable Development Goals or Global Goals are a collection of 17 interlinked global goals designed to be a "blueprint to achieve a better and more sustainable future for all." The SDGs were set in 2015 by the United Nations General Assembly and are intended to be achieved by the year 2030.

SUSTAINABLE INVESTING

One outcome of the move toward sustainability and stakeholder capitalism is a shift in investing focus. ESG-related investment vehicles, commonly referred to as sustainable investing, have emerged and are gaining popularity. Jon Hale of Morningstar provides an excellent way to understand the term sustainable investing and its relationship to ESG:

> Sustainable investing is a range of investment approaches that put the analysis of environmental, social, and governance, or ESG, criteria at the center of the process used to evaluate investments, build portfolios, and assess their societal impact. The use of ESG criteria is grounded in materiality and, at a minimum, contributes to a more thorough financial analysis at a time when corporate performance on sustainability issues is under greater scrutiny by a range of stakeholders. Sustainable investing

*supports the notion of stakeholder value — the idea that the
purpose of the corporation is to create sustainable value for all of
its stakeholders over the long term. It encourages more-responsible corporate behavior, which results in firms reducing negative
externalities, helps them attract and retain a competitive workforce, enhances their intangible value, and strengthens confidence in the overall financial system. Sustainable investing also
encourages direct investment in areas like renewable energy and
green technologies as the world transitions to a low-carbon
economy.*[27]

Sustainable investment options are widely accepted in Europe and
gaining traction in the United States. Flows into sustainable funds totaled
$21.4 billion in 2019, a nearly four-fold increase over the previous calendar
year record.[28] The number of conventional investment funds considering
ESG factors has also increased significantly, growing from 81 in 2018 to
564 in 2019; in 2019, sustainable funds outperformed their conventional
peers.[29]

Despite these positive results, there is marked resistance to the adoption of sustainable investing practices for employee pension and retirement
funds. After a proposed DoL rule that would govern how the almost $11
trillion invested in private pension plans should be managed, Eugene
Scalia, U.S. Secretary of Labor (and son of the late Supreme Court Justice
Antonin Scalia) eschewed the idea that pension investors might do-well-
and-do-good. In an opinion piece for the *Wall Street Journal,* he said,

*ESG investing poses particular concerns under the Employee
Retirement Income Security Act, or ERISA, the federal law governing private retirement plans. At the heart of ERISA is the
requirement that plan fiduciaries act with an "eye single" to
funding the retirements of plan participants and beneficiaries.
This means investment decisions must be based solely on whether*

they enhance retirement savings, regardless of the fiduciary's personal preferences. The department's proposed rule reminds plan providers that it is unlawful to sacrifice returns, or accept additional risk, through investments intended to promote a social or political end.[30]

TRANSPARENCY

Transparency refers to the extent to which shareholders, investors and other stakeholders have ready access to a company's or a market's data, such as audited financial reports, market depth, price levels, and the planned actions and behaviors of its senior management. At their heart, stakeholder or inclusive capitalism, sustainability, and integrated reporting are all built upon ideals of increased and meaningful transparency.

CHAPTER 4

The Challenges of Measurement

"Align yourself to drive what society needs and expects from you or you'll become obsolete."

— BRIAN MOYNIHAN, CEO OF BANK OF AMERICA AND CHAIR, INTERNATIONAL BUSINESS COUNCIL OF THE WORLD ECONOMIC FORUM

PETER DRUCKER ONCE SAID, "WHAT GETS MEASURED GETS managed." Data point us in a new, positive and potentially more profitable direction. It is a long-overdue step toward accounting for the value created and destroyed through people practices in our businesses. A growing body of research is documenting and proving how critical the workforce is to value creation. One study from the London School of Business, for instance, found employee engagement and satisfaction correlates directly to company performance. This specific study found the 100 Best Companies to Work for in America delivered stock returns that beat their peers by an average of 2.3 to 3.8% per year over a 28-year period (89% to 184% cumulative).[31] Essentially, this research points to the importance of People Economics, the concept we introduced in the last chapter.

Ironically, the role of people is becoming even more pronounced amid technological change. McKinsey & Company identified the most-important factors in effecting digital transformation as related to whether an organization either has or can develop the requisite talent and skillsets.[32] Digital transformation, especially in a world gone remote, represents one of business's most-important continuity and growth levers; it underscores the risks of overlooking HCM. Owners and investors who perceive advances in artificial intelligence (AI) and machine learning to automate and cut their way to growth are doing it wrong.

Research is also proving out the benefits of cognitive diversity in the workforce — and it is not just emanating from academia. Recent analysis from Morgan Stanley, for instance, found globally, the most gender-diverse companies outperformed their peers by 3.1% per annum between 2010 and 2019.[33] In the U.S., opportunities for this kind of performance are in peril as COVID-19's disproportionate impact on women workers becomes increasingly evident.[34]

Still, the risk of ignoring ESG and HCM considerations often fails to hit home until it is too late. For instance, in testimony before Congress, Boeing's CEO had to explain why he ignored repeated warnings from employees concerned about the safety of the aircraft-maker's Super Max plane. The CEO was confronted by one email, sent directly to him, that suggested fatigue and "schedule pressure" were contributing to worker mistakes and decisions to circumvent established processes. Yet, Boeing made no changes to its production schedule. For those keeping score, its market cap had lost in excess of $54 billion after the second crash involving the company's Super Max plane, as of October 30, the day of the hearings.

Almost all executives claim their people are the most-important asset of their company. Some would argue it has become a cliché. Yet, from a financial standpoint, employees are only recognized as an expense line on the balance sheet, bundled in with "other" intangible items. This not only conceals the impact of people in driving company growth but also characterizes employees solely as a cost.

Experience has taught us that businesses both large and small are underinvested in human capital capabilities and the HR function. The mere mention of HR causes people to roll their eyes, snort with derision and share stories of the insufferable nature of an HR professional they had the misfortune of working with. It is quite possible they have gotten what they have paid for. Indeed, many organizations lack solid people processes, practices and technologies, and dedicated HR staff, which makes measurement and reporting a virtual impossibility. It also hampers the ability to create value. You cannot manage what you do not measure.

Contrary to outdated accounting principles, you *can* measure the value and contribution of your employees. One of the biggest advances in HCM and ESG has been the development of new metrics that re-orient analysis to focus on the latent opportunity within the workforce. In HCM, for instance, more-sophisticated programs measure the return on human capital investments or track the total cost of the workforce (TCOW) as a percentage of operating expenses. Investors, meanwhile, have begun looking at productivity of workers (versus profits alone) as a driver of value. In ESG, alternatively, relevant metrics might include days lost to illness per full-time employee or statistics for gender balance and diversity throughout the organization.

Some investors have taken great pains to track and even publish these figures, highlighting their role in addressing these social factors and emphasizing the impact on the stability of the companies under their watch. Apax Partners, for instance, publishes an ESG report that also tracks the percentage of its companies with health and safety policies, anti-corruption guidelines, environmental and waste management protocols, and supply-chain transparency at the portfolio company level.[35] Bank of America produces comprehensive reporting as part of its commitment to transparency, including an annual Human Capital Management Report.[36]

Still, the terms HR and HCM are often conflated. In the process, organizations overlook the material impact HCM strategies can have on workforce productivity, company performance and ultimately fund-level returns for investors. Quite simply, they overlook People Alpha.

You see, it is one thing to know what's material and what isn't; it is another to track and measure progress. None of this will create the desired impact without following through. This should go without saying, but in our experience, the impact is often far greater than most anticipate. The importance of transparency also cannot be understated. In a vacuum, employees will let their imaginations get the best of them. Trust, however, translates into a healthy workforce, higher retention, productivity gains and ultimately financial performance. As Klaus Schwab, founder and executive chair of the WEF, says, "Trust will come from proven ESG performance."[37]

CRIES FOR TRANSPARENCY

Transparency is a critical issue for investors and stakeholders of every stripe. In his 2019 letter to CEOs, Larry Fink said:

> ... I believe we are on the edge of a fundamental reshaping of finance. ... As I have written in past letters, a company cannot achieve long-term profits without embracing purpose and considering the needs of a broad range of stakeholders. ... Given the groundwork we have already laid engaging on disclosure, and the growing investment risks surrounding sustainability, we will be increasingly disposed to vote against management and board directors when companies are not making sufficient progress on sustainability-related disclosures and the business practices and plans underlying them.[38]

Investors *do* believe this information would be of use to them. That understanding the mechanisms of value creation is important — important enough to petition the SEC to require their disclosure.[39] The constituencies are out of step with one another, although progress is being made to align them. Over the last few years, several organizations have pushed for greater insight into and measurement of human capital, especially in publicly traded companies. The argument is shareholders and institutions should have access to all information that is *material* (i.e., important to the outcomes of the individual business), and that human capital is typically a black box. The SEC recently announced the modernization of Regulation S-K, which requires public companies to disclose material aspects of human capital activity.

In his August 26, 2020, announcement regarding the modernization of Reg S-K, Jay Clayton, chair of the SEC said:

> *I fully support the requirement in today's rules that companies must describe their human capital resources, including any human capital measures or objectives they focus on in managing the business, to the extent material to an understanding of the company's business as a whole. From a modernization stand-point, today, human capital accounts for and drives long-term business value in many companies much more so than it did 30 years ago. Today's rules reflect that important and multifaceted shift in our domestic and global economy.*[40]

You may say to yourself, "I am a private company or an investor in private companies so none of this applies to me." True, the SEC ruling and the recently passed House Bill H.R. 5930, Workforce Investment Disclosure Act of 2020,[41] do not apply to private organizations. However, if you have an interest in making an initial public offering (IPO) or you are investing funds that have been raised from limited partners who are also members of the HCMC,[42] among others, you will eventually be asked to account for your human capital practices.

More and more, stakeholders are looking at companies' people prac-tices as indicators of their ethics, values and integrity. For example, con-sumers make buying decisions; prospective employees make career choices; and partners, affiliates, vendors, suppliers and contractors choose whom to associate with based on reputation. You need look no further than Glassdoor, Rate My Professor or Angi for confirmation.

What is getting in the way of measurement and reporting? Paul Washington of the Conference Board says, "[T]ime and attention at the board and senior executive levels [needs to be allocated] to think through … the workforce you have now and what is the workforce you [will] need in the future to achieve your objectives — this is required to tell your story to the investors, which will also require [reliable data]."[43]

Washington recommends recent Prudential and Lockheed Martin proxies as good examples of public company disclosures. For these examples and others, take a look at Appendix B.

MEASUREMENT: A CAUTIONARY TALE

In an era where measurement and data are the tools of transparency, it would be very easy to slide down the slippery slope yet again. In a *Harvard Business Review* article, Peter Cappelli reminds us to remain vigilant and adopt a balanced approach:

> *While many organizations — especially ones that are flatter or have adopted agile methods — still claim to believe that engaged employees matter, a significant and rising number seem to be following an optimization approach, wherein decision-making and control are pushed back to experts and algorithms. Labor is treated as a commodity, and the goal is to cut it to a minimum by replacing employees with contract and gig workers and by using automation and software to reduce the need for human judgment. Ideal behaviors are dictated to the remaining employees, who are closely monitored for compliance. So far, this change has not been backed up by evidence that it's an improvement.*
>
> *Optimization appeals to most executives because they've been taught how to do it and understand it. History suggests, though, that knock-on problems caused by seeing worker productivity solely as an engineering challenge have been enormous and persistent. So we should know better this time around. Generations*

of evidence about the benefits of employee empowerment and the costs of taking it away are being ignored. It is possible to strike a balance between the two models and get benefits from both, but that requires backing away from the idea that worker performance is fundamentally an engineering issue.[44]

PEOPLE ARE NOT ASSETS

We are at a crossroads and the proverbial road-less-traveled beckons. The imbalanced understanding of the value of people in business has led to an imperfect calculus. Despite the statements by CEOs that people are their most important asset, the fact remains that as far as U.S. accounting standards are concerned, *people are not an asset at all.* GAAP accounting standards don't classify employees as assets; instead, they guide corporate accountants to incorporate staffing costs along with other intangible assets into one, all-encompassing expense line on the balance sheet. In an odd twist of fate, dollars spent on wages, salaries, benefits, training and development are categorized as expenses, and dollars spent on restroom repairs are considered leasehold or capital improvements.

To flesh this out a bit, there are somewhat competing financial standards in use — GAAP in the United States, and IFRS outside the U.S. GAAP is viewed as a rules-based system of accounting, and the IFRS a principles-based system. For our purposes, we will only look at their differing definitions of the term "asset."

GAAP defines an asset as "a future economic benefit," whereas the IFRS framework defines an asset as "a resource from which future economic benefit will flow to a company."[45] While the differences may seem semantic, they are important and point to one of the explanations for why the United States has been resistant to adopting a full view of the value of and accounting for intangible assets, such as human capital. Other parts of the world have embraced or are in the process of embracing a more holistic view.

Then there is the question of tangible versus intangible assets. Tangible assets are items that have a physical form and hold value. Typical items include property; plant and equipment; and cash, inventory, accounts receivable and investments; they can be seen and felt, destroyed by accidents, disaster, fires and floods. As discussed, intangible assets generally lack physical form and include things such as intellectual property, copyrights, trademarks, brands, patents and goodwill.

Why is this important? In 2018, the intangible value of the five biggest companies on the S&P 500 index was $21.03 trillion USD. During the same year, that value of tangible assets was only $4 trillion. In contrast, the five biggest companies on the S&P 500 index in 1985 had $1 trillion in tangible asset value with an intangible value of roughly half that amount.[46]Take a look at the following chart.[47]If intangible assets now comprise 90 percent of the value of the largest S&P 500 companies and they are made up of items that are neither captured on a balance sheet nor accounted for as assets, how are they being measured? More importantly, how are they being cared for, cultivated, grown and preserved? This is precisely why one of these intangibles — human capital — is the subject of this book.

Ocean Tomo has released an interim update to the Annual Study of Intangible Asset Market Value (IAMV). The study examines the components of market value, specifically the role of intangible assets across a range of global indexes. In this update, IAMV is calculated by subtracting net tangible asset value from market capitalization.

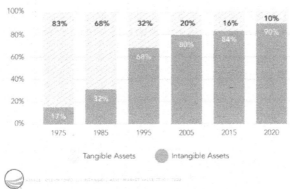

COMPONENTS OF S&P 500 MARKET VALUE

CREATING REPORTING FRAMEWORKS

There are an abundance of reporting frameworks, recommended metrics and measures. The topography is changing and efforts at creating a more coherent and unified set of disclosure expectations is underway. One organization leading the charge is the IBC of the WEF. The IBC describes itself as a "global organization committed to advancing global economies by fostering business and leadership development opportunities amongst governments and businesses worldwide" and comprises CEOs from more than 130 of the world's largest and most-respected companies. Working in coordination with the Big Four professional services firms (Ernst & Young [EY], PricewaterhouseCoopers [PwC], Deloitte and KPMG), the IBC and others are attempting to reconcile the various ESG reporting frameworks and establish a minimum standard set of reporting metrics; essentially an ESG disclosure roadmap. The key is to establish standard metrics, which make it easier to compare organization-to-organization and year-over-year data, ostensibly offering insight into organizational progress and performance.

The consortium aims to achieve universal adoption among their members in their first-tier implementation, followed rapidly with adoption by organizations who are members of the Business Roundtable, which is made up of CEOs of leading, primarily U.S. companies, representing more than 15 million employees and more than $7 trillion in revenues (as of 2018). Responding to the IBC/WEF's consultation draft, "Toward Common Metrics and Consistent Reporting of Sustainable Value Creation,"[48] the International Federation of Accountants (IFAC) said:

> "Alignment, harmonization, and convergence must take place before regional or jurisdiction-specific initiatives create fragmentation that becomes standard practice—impeding the goal of consistent reporting of relevant, reliable, and comparable information. ... Leaders in the accountancy profession must also collaborate and find areas of agreement."[49]

SETTING TRADITIONAL STANDARDS

Responsibility for defining traditional financial reporting standards in the United States, including definitions of terms such as assets and standards of materiality, falls principally to two entities: FASB and GASB. FASB takes as its mission "to establish and improve financial accounting and reporting standards to provide useful information to investors and other users of financial reports; and educate stakeholders on how to most effectively understand and implement those standards."

Established in 1973, FASB is an independent nonprofit organization with responsibility for setting accounting standards for United States companies and nonprofits. The SEC views FASB as the accounting standard-setter for public companies. FASB works with the IASB to establish compatible standards around the globe. FASB's sister organization, GASB, was established in 1984 and has similar responsibilities for state and local governments. Together, the IASB and FASB have oversight for the IFRS and GAAP standards, respectively.

The United States' GAAP and the IFRS establish sets of common terms, definitions and calculations that keep accounting practices consistent mong businesses and industries. Although GAAP standards are not law, violations of GAAP can result in credibility issues with lenders, investors and prospective acquirers. For publicly traded organizations, failure to meet accounting standards may result in significant monetary penalties from the SEC, poor investment analyst ratings, destruction of consumer and employee trust, loss of share value, and the potential for shareholder lawsuits.

As an example, let's take a closer look at how the IFRS defines materiality, which we briefly discussed in the previous chapter. "Information is material if omitting, misstating or obscuring it could reasonably be expected to influence decisions that the primary users of a specific [organization's] general purpose financial statements make on the basis of those financial statements."[50] In layperson's terms, this means sharing or not sharing information that affects your decision-making is material.

The IFRS also asks reporting organizations to consider magnitude of materiality, meaning details that may influence opinions but not in a substantial way. For example, while we may not appreciate an organization's individual choice on a matter, knowing the detail wouldn't sway our decision to invest taken as a whole. Materiality is entity-specific. Using the example of a pharmaceutical company, quality is a material issue for patients, prescribers and investors. Stakeholders want to know a pharmaceutical company's products are safe and effective, comply with established Good Manufacturing (GMP) and Good Laboratory Processes (GLPs), and have passed all required Food and Drug Administration (FDA) inspections without negative findings. Investors want to invest in an organization that is responsible and ethical in its commitment to maintaining the highest standards of science and manufacturing. Certainly, issues of quality would influence an investor's choices.

SETTING NEW STANDARDS

The array of reporting measures and various regulated reporting requirements, especially those for public companies, is indeed astounding. Yet, as we've already touched on, transparency is rapidly becoming table stakes for both public and private companies. Stakeholders, specifically investors, are looking for greater and more-detailed insight into the material aspects of the organizations in which they invest. Demand for this insight transcends public organizations and now includes disclosures regarding private organizations, including those being invested in through fund commitments to alternative asset investors such as private equity and hedge funds.

Many of these investors recognize the importance of ESG-related items and are looking for standardized, comparable accountability measures, beyond an organization's annual statement or social media posts about their corporate social responsibility (CSR) activities. As an example, the lack of available, rigorously derived data has led institutional investors to use Glassdoor ratings alone to evaluate the people practices of would-be investments.

However, several organizations are setting standards for our changing world. The SASB, established in 2011, has a mission to "establish industry-specific disclosure standards across ESG topics that facilitate communication between companies and investors about material, decision-useful information. Such information should be relevant, reliable and comparable on a global basis." SASB has developed a set of 77 globally applicable, industry-specific standards that "identify the minimal set of financially material sustainability topics and their associated metrics for the typical company in an industry."[51] SASB standards and an interactive materiality matrix, alongside a host of additional resources, are available at www.sasb.org. These tools serve as a comprehensive taxonomy for defining and determining materiality which, when viewed in their entirety, may feel overwhelming.

As in the case of the UN SDGs, each organization will have to align business purpose, strategic goals, operating objectives and intended ESG impact against the recommended reporting guidelines to determine which measures apply to their own unique situation. None of the available frameworks are intended to be adopted in totality. In the case of the SASB guidelines, for example, application of the materiality matrix can focus and simplify a business's reporting and disclosure.

The Principles for Responsible Investing (PRI) were established in 2011 by the United Nations and the OECD. In response to expectations from broad stakeholder constituencies, the PRI sets out a mandate for institutional investors (organizations responsible for investing money on behalf of other people) and businesses to respect human rights. The PRI provides "six Principles for Responsible Investment [which] are a voluntary and aspirational set of investment principles that offer a menu of possible actions for incorporating ESG issues into investment practice."[52]

Signatories commit to:

1. Incorporating ESG issues into their investment analysis and decision-making processes

2. Being active owners and incorporating ESG issues into their own ownership policies and practices

3. Seeking appropriate disclosure on ESG issues by the entities in which they invest

4. Promoting acceptance and implementation of the Principles within the investment industry

5. Working together to enhance their effectiveness in implementing the Principles

6. Reporting on their activities and progress toward implementing the Principles

PRI signatories invest in private equity, hedge funds, infrastructure, real estate, farmland and forestry. PRI reported 3,038 signatories representing more than $100 trillion USD in assets as of their 2019/2020 reporting period, a global increase of 28% over the previous reporting period. United States signatories represent 587, or just under 20%, of the global signatories.

Earlier, we looked at the definitional differences between GAAP and IFRS. A manifestation of these linguistic, and therefore practical, differences can be seen in voluntary reporting via PRI participation. As discussed, United States accounting principles have historically failed to account for intangibles (e.g., human capital, brands, knowledge, etc.) as assets. Outside the U.S., businesses and regulators have adopted a broader and more-encompassing view. Frankly, the U.S. is behind our global colleagues in recognizing and disclosing the components of value creation (and depletion).

Organizations such as Ceres,[53] an investor-led sustainability nonprofit, are working with scientists, policymakers and activists around the world to advance efforts at institutional transparency. The GRI is one such outcome. Founded in 1997 after the Exxon Valdez oil spill, the GRI exists "to help organizations be transparent and take responsibility for their impacts so that we can create a sustainable future."[54] Their mechanism for doing so is to create a global common language for organizational reporting.

Another effort, led by the United Auto Workers Retiree Medical Benefits Trust, is the HCMC,[55] a cooperative effort of 32 diverse influential institutional investors, representing more than $6 trillion USD in assets.

The coalition has come together to "elevate human capital management as a critical component in company performance."[56] In 2017, the HCMC petitioned the SEC to spur changes to require United States public company disclosures on human capital metrics. Their efforts succeeded, resulting in the adoption of human capital reporting requirements in the SEC's Regulation S-K Modernization ruling.

TOWARD NEW STANDARD METRICS

A significant criticism of the SEC's ruling has been the lack of standard metrics and measures to guide the required disclosures. An abundance of potential ESG and specific human capital reporting frameworks exist. The SASB, GRI, and PRI principles are just the beginning. Many of the existing frameworks and recommended measures inform each other and are complementary; others are confusing and contradictory. Efforts are underway seeking to distill and clarify reporting requirements and investor responsibilities, headed by the various framework developers as well as regulators and policymakers. Most notably, in September 2020, GRI, IIRC, SASB, and other groups pledged to work together to provide guidance and develop a shared vision of how together these standards complement established financial principles.[57] In the next chapter, we will take a closer look at the <IR> Framework, developed by the International Integrated Reporting Council (IIRC).

Early work to develop integrated standards includes a "Four Pillar Approach"[58] adopted by the WEF and the Big Four accounting firms. The pillars are 1) Governance, 2) Planet, 3) People, and 4) Prosperity. They use existing ESG standards to map 21 core and 34 expanded metrics to the UN Sustainable Development Goals. Companies are encouraged to report or explain issues material to long-term value creation; their ESG performance; and impacts of business operations on the planet and in society, as stated at the Summer 2020 IBC/World Economic Forum.

1. **Principles of governance:** how purpose is embedded across the company; progress against strategic milestones; remuneration; alignment of strategy and policies to lobbying; monetary impacts of unethical behavior; consideration of economic, environmental, and social issues in capital allocation

2. **Planet:** aligning greenhouse gas (GHG) targets to the Paris Agreement; impact of GHG emissions; land use of operations and full supply chain; impact of land use and conversion on ecosystems; impact of water consumption and withdrawal; air pollution and its impact; water pollution and its impact; single-use plastics in the value chain; impact of solid waste disposal; resource circularity

3. **People:** pay gap percentages; discrimination and harassment incidents and corresponding monetary losses; percentage of workforce and suppliers under collective bargaining agreements; human rights reviews, grievance impact, and modern slavery; living wage percentage; monetary impact of work-related incidents; employee well-being statistics; number of unfilled skilled positions; monetary impacts of employee training

4. **Prosperity:** infrastructure investments and services and the indirect economic impacts; society value-generated percentage; vitality index; total social investments; additional tax remitted; total tax paid by country for significant locations

A NEW DEFINITION OF SUCCESS

Each of us has an individual yardstick by which to measure and determine our degree of accomplishment or failure. It could be the amount of savings in your individual retirement account; number of hours you've been able to volunteer this year; or amount of the principal on your mortgage you have reduced. Like each individual, every business has its own definition of success, generally linked to an overarching strategy, and reduced to a set of business goals and objectives.

Goals and objectives are sometimes referred to as key performance indicators (KPIs) and measured by sales or growth revenue. We would all agree this is a critically important company-level measure of accomplishment. When broken down into details like sales per division, sales per customer or sales per product, the details help to identify the type and nature of revenue generation. Sales figures are also helpful when compared over periods of time, such as year-over-year, quarter-over-quarter or month-over-month. Generally, some revenue indicator is used as a goal or objective of every going concern.

KPIs differ, however, in interest and importance by industry, organization and stakeholder. JUST Capital's issues survey, referenced earlier in this chapter, provides direct evidence of what matters to some Americans. In a world where multi-stakeholder views are gaining in prominence, understanding upfront what matters to whom and factoring these perspectives into your organization's or team's definitions of success is essential.

Let's look at this from a shareholder perspective. Imagine a pharmaceutical company launching a new dermatology product. Executives, shareholders, customers, prescribers, government regulators and employees each have particular views about what matters. Some of their concerns are the same; some are complementary; and others may seem contradictory. Success comes in understanding, accounting for and addressing all these views and demands holistically and simultaneously.

Executives	Shareholders	Customers	Prescribing Physicians	Regulators (U.S. FDA)	Employees
Sales Revenue	Sales Revenue	Quality (Safe/Effective)	Quality (Safe/Effective)	Quality (Safe/Effective)	Sales Revenue
Market / Market share	Quality (Safe and effective)	Affordable	Availability	Few/No Unwanted Side Effects	Quality (Safe/Effective)
Cost to Produce	Market/Market Share	Easily Used & Well Tolerated	Easily Used & Well Tolerated	Meets Required Manufacturing and Laboratory Standards	Easily Manufactured

As we have seen, investors come in various types and sizes. Some will have deep levels of financial, managerial and emotional commitment to a business — perhaps yours. You'll recall investors (shareholders) are only one set of stakeholders with an interest in business operations. Many of these stakeholders are clamoring for a peek inside. It is this multi-stakeholder perspective that informs integrated thinking, which the IIRC defines as:

> ... the active consideration by an organization of the relationships between its various operating and functional units and the capitals that the organization uses or affects. Integrated thinking leads to integrated decision-making and actions that consider the creation of value over the short, medium and long term. Integrated thinking takes into account the connectivity and interdependencies between the range of factors that affect an organization's ability to create value over time, including the capitals that the organization uses or affects, and the critical interdependencies, including tradeoffs, between them; the capacity of the organization to respond to key stakeholders' legitimate needs and interests, how the organization tailors its business model and strategy to respond to its external environment and the risks and opportunities it faces; and organization's activities,

performance (financial and other) and outcomes in terms of the
capitals — past, present and future.[59]

The accounting profession is also seeing a need for and advocating change. In a joint white paper published in June 2020, IFAC and the American Institute of Certified Public Accountants (AICPA) stated, "While accounting for the balance sheet will always remain important, not least in preparing for and managing through difficult times, performance and value cannot be adequately captured and measured in financial terms by the balance sheet or by financial shareholder metrics. Success requires creating and demonstrating value for all stakeholders, not just shareholders, and addressing societal expectations related to sustainability and broader impact."[60]

Following along the road-less-traveled, the Davos Manifesto 2020 said: "The purpose of a company is to engage all its stakeholders in shared and sustained value creation. ... A company treats its people with dignity and respect. It honours diversity and strives for continuous improvements in working conditions and employee well-being. In a world of rapid change, a company fosters continued employability through ongoing upskilling and reskilling."[61]

CHAPTER 5

Accounting for Human Capital: A Blended Standards Model

"Our merchants and masters complain much of the bad effects of high wages in raising the price and lessening the sale of goods. They say nothing concerning the bad effects of high profits. They are silent with regard to the pernicious effects of their own gains. They complain only of those of other people."

— ADAM SMITH, *THE THEORY OF MORAL SENTIMENTS*

DO YOU REMEMBER THE SCENE IN "THE WIZARD OF OZ" where Toto pulls back the curtain on the wizard and we see him pulling levers, twisting dials, pushing buttons and generally working the magic of the Emerald City? As a business owner, leader or investor, you are your own wizard by design or default. Higher sales, larger revenues, customer retention and stock price are all realized or depleted by your manipulations of the levers, dials and buttons. While historically we looked to tools like business process optimization, lean six sigma and scientific management to guide our efforts, by themselves, they are insufficient to get us where we need to be when it comes to human capital.

The problem is all these tools treat people as a process component, and not as a value driver. In reality, unique organizational value is built upon the components and their interplay, including the often-missing human capital elements. Taking this whole systems view is the basis for the integrated thinking approach introduced earlier, and equally important, the way investors are beginning to look at the value of their investments. As articulated by SEC Chairman Jay Clayton in 2019: "Today, human capital and intellectual property often represent an essential resource and driver of performance for many companies. This is a shift from human capital being viewed, at least from an income statement perspective, as a cost."[62]

How does Alpha play out in sustainability investing, which is also referred to as impact investing? In the 2018 report entitled "The Alpha in Impact: How operating with an impact objective can add financial value for investors," Tideline and the Impact Capital Managers defined Impact Alpha as "the ways in which operating with an impact objective enhances investment management and adds financial value for investors, fund managers, and their investees."[63] Their construct discusses three types of investment and operating activities comprising 10 drivers that include attracting and retaining manager and investee talent, leveraging impact expertise to develop more effective businesses, and promoting discipline and efficiency through impact accountability.

UNDERSTANDING PEOPLE ALPHA

The idea of People Alpha based on accounting for human capital is not a new concept. It can be traced to the 1970s, about the same time as the creation of international accounting standard (IAS) 38, Milton Friedman's famous *New York Times* essay and the original Davos Manifesto. Human resources accounting (HRA), also called human capital accounting (HCA), is built on principles and theories of corporate valuation and human capital metrics. The earliest of these is attributed to Nicholas Flamholtz, who in 1972 argued, "The value of human capital (HC) to the organization is the present value of all future services that [a person] is expected to provide during the period that he/she remains in the organization."[64]

In 1978, Jac Fitz-Enz, regarded as the father of human resources metrics, published an article titled "The Measurement Imperative" in which he proposed human resources activities and their impact on the bottom line could be measured.[65] Since then, the human resources community has argued that HR analytics can help organizations address strategic and tactical competitive challenges. Fitz-Enz made meaningful contributions to the human resources community; his HR metrics consultancy, the Saratoga Institute, was eventually sold to PricewaterhouseCoopers.

Calls to account for and disclose human capital and intangible assets as components of corporate valuation are relatively recent. Using current accounting standards, investments in intangible assets are either immediately expensed in financial statements or arbitrarily amortized and therefore are not fully reflected on the balance sheet. As a result, book values of firms with a significant amount of human capital and other intangible asset investments are unrelated to their market values. Despite the difficulty in measurement, as contributors to the creation of economic value added (EVA), it is crucial to know the value of human capital, to be able to provide more realistic financial statements and to manage human resources efficiently. In their joint paper about problems in human resources accounting, Rahaman, Hossain and Akter (2013) make this eloquent argument for human capital measures.

> *Assets are resources from which future economic value will flow to the entity. As an employee of an organization will not merely work for a single year, it seems rational to account for [an] employee as an asset [o]n the balance sheet on the ground[s] that they will provide future economic benefit to the entity. ... The movement toward fair value accounting seen in recent years for international standards indicates a more sophisticated approach to the measurement of assets, tangible as well as intangible.*[66]

Human capital accounting and human resources metrics represent two parallel and largely academic debates that have smoldered for more than four decades — a spark without a flame. These debates continue and until recently, there has been little cause to bridge the divide. Today's firms invest heavily in intangible assets, including human capital, which is acquired with the expectation it will generate future revenues. That means including human capital information in published financial statements "would, in all likelihood, make such statements f[a]r more meaningful in predicting future performance, which is of course, the principal concern of investors," said Jawahar Lal, former dean of the Delhi School of Economics.[67]

To address these concerns and opportunities, the two worlds have to come together. Unfortunately, we are using two independent languages and multiple frameworks to capture, define and discuss the same concepts. The HR community looks to the International Standards Organization (ISO) and to Fitz-Enz and Donald Kirkpatrick's (1959) model of training evaluation to inform their vocabulary, while the finance and accounting profession have adopted GRI, the Embankment Project for Inclusive Capitalism (EPIC), IIRC, and other terms and definitions. Solid HR metrics, such as those initially developed by Fitz-Enz and Kirkpatrick coupled with accounting standards, valuation formulae and integrated reporting, are all necessary components of a holistic approach to understanding the worth attributable to people in our businesses. Illustrations of this divide and suggestions for a holistic approach, or at least recognition of the gaps, will be covered in the following sections.

As with every other business function today, data and analytics are revolutionizing how organizations measure and track key performance indicators related to employees and business performance. Analytics not only provide a baseline to measure the state of a company's human capital, but also provide mechanisms to continually optimize human capital management strategies based on evolving objectives and changes to the market or economy. Steven Sheffrin argues human capital may be categorized into two types. "Human as labor force is the economic added-value generated by the input of labor force similar to elements such as financial capital, land, machinery and labor hours" while "human as creator" frames knowledge, skills, competency and experience originated by continuously connecting between self and environment. When these are combined, "... human capital is the stock of skills and knowledge embodied in the ability to perform labor so as to produce economic value."[68] Over the years, a proliferation of calculations, definitions and frameworks has emerged to measure and optimize human capital contributions to business. As you will see, there is still work to be done to create universally accepted standards; nonetheless, recent work is building on the strengths of past efforts and seeks to find common ground among the various constituencies.

ENTER THE ISO 30414 AND THE PEOPLE PILLAR

ISO 30414 Human Resource Management Guidelines for Internal and External Human Capital Reporting[69] is the standard developed by the ISO to enable organizations to understand their impact on staff better and maximize employee contributions for long-term success. Finalized and released in November 2018, ISO 30414 is a long-awaited validation of the importance of human capital measurement. Comprising 60 metrics in 11 core areas, ISO 30414 tracks measures of compliance and ethics; diversity; leadership; organizational culture; wellbeing, health and safety; costs; productivity; recruitment/mobility and turnover; skills and capability; succession planning; and workforce availability. ISO's guidelines, ISO 30415 Human Resource Management—Diversity and Inclusion,[70] does the same for measures of diversity, equality and inclusion.

In his 2019 response to the SEC's request for comments about the proposal to modernize Regulation S-K, Lee Webster, founder and first chair of the ISO Human Capital Technical Working Group said the ISO 30414 standards "rest on a foundation of trusted and comparable methods to calculate metrics ... by promoting measures comprised of simple, commonly known algorithms; ... describe the workforce subjects unambiguously; ... and can be replicated by any organization wishing to determine the same information."[71]

The ISO standards fit nicely within existing integrated reporting models such as the <IR> Framework introduced earlier. They also provide an essential ingredient in establishing sustainability accounting standards for human capital, as are being developed by SASB and the organizations collaborating on the IBC/WEF metrics initiative. However, metrics such as the ISO 30414 standards are not enough. Beyond just quantifying the role of people, metrics such as human capital return on investment (ROI) can help to re-orient CEOs, CFOs and GPs to think of employees not as an expense, but as an opportunity for investment with a payoff.

Earlier we introduced the WEF/IBC Stakeholder metrics framework and its four pillars: Government, Planet, People and Prosperity. Within each of these pillars are themes "that provide high-level concepts and direction relevant to good governance and that enable companies to take a holistic and tailored approach to the information they provide." Basically guidelines for structured reporting, each of these themes contains guidance and direction for reporting standards and metrics. The WEF/IBC metrics related to human capital largely draw from GRI and EPIC.

As an aside, the WEF/IBC people metrics ignore ISO 30414, ISO 30415, OSHA and other traditional human resources reporting metrics (Appendix A provides comparison tables to illustrate this point). This is another example of the bifurcation of HR, finance and regulatory requirements via language, terminology and thinking — a chasm, albeit unintentional, between parallel functions with ostensibly common missions. Communication, understanding and value creation rest on having a common language and operating definitions from which to engage in discourse and debate. Until we cross this divide, we will continue to operate at cross purposes with one another. People — your greatest asset — falls through the crack.

Despite this lack of connection to ISO 30414, ISO 30415, OSHA and other reporting metrics, the WEF/IBC People Pillar provides an important framework, clearly linked to several of the UN SDG goals: 1) No Poverty; 3) Good Health and Well-Being; 4) Quality Education; 5) Gender Equality, 8) Decent Work and Economic Growth, and 10) Reduced Inequalities. As stated in the introduction to the People Pillar:

People are crucial for every organization; their growth—in knowledge, prosperity and well-being — is central to the success of all organizations and societies. The business case for firms to measure, manage and disclose information on how they ensure an engaged, skilled and healthy workforce across their value chains is compelling. Such a workforce creates both financial and non-financial value that is critical for a company's business performance and competitive advantage, while enabling it to mitigate risks, maintain a licence to operate and strengthen stakeholder relationships.[72]

FRAMING THE DISCUSSION

I have used the WEF/IBC Common Metrics and Consistent Reporting Standards to frame this discussion of accounting for human capital. I will use their theme definitions and augment them with others as necessary to foster deeper meaning, highlight important differences in approach and bridge gaps in understanding.

I have quoted extensively and precisely from the standards to give you the exact language. It will be italicized. The associated metrics and disclosures for these themes include core and expanded metrics. Core metrics are intended to be the minimum standard set of disclosures for all organizations. Expanded metrics are considered supplemental and are recommended for increased transparency and where disclosure of these items would be considered material for the industry and individual organization. See Appendix A for detailed use of core and expanded metrics and disclosures.

The three themes I focus on here are:

- Dignity and Equality

- Health and Well-Being

- Skills for the Future

According to the WEF/IBC Common Metrics and Consistent Reporting Standards on Dignity and Equality:

This theme focuses on providing equitable opportunities to all employees in recruitment and selection, training, development and promotion. These opportunities should remain unaffected by their gender, race, age, ethnicity, ability and sexual orientation, in a workplace where all employees feel valued and respected and receive fair treatment with appropriate compensations and benefits. By embracing diversity and equal opportunities, companies can help integrate under-represented groups and minorities into the labour market, so they become a better reflection of society and also deepen the pool of talent that a more diverse workforce can bring.[73]

According to the WEF/IBC Common Metrics and Consistent Reporting Standards on Health and Well-Being:

This theme requires organizations to ensure the health, safety, and mental, physical and social well-being of all people in their operations and value chains. ... Companies that maintain high standards in health, safety and labour rights can see higher levels of employee productivity and operations efficiency. Working proactively in these areas of the business will help identify and mitigate risks — and it is increasingly required by law.[74]

According to the WEF/IBC Common Metrics and Consistent Reporting Standards on Skills for the Future:

Access to skilled workers is a key factor in becoming a successful company. To address the skills-gap challenge, companies must increase investment in training, educating and reskilling their workforce to grasp the opportunities of changing work patterns due to new tools and technologies. Today's businesses should aim to equip people with the skills they need to innovate and thereby create jobs and prosperity, measured in both financial and human capital.[75]

CHAPTER 6

Measuring Organizational Culture

"Good management is largely a matter of love ... a sacred trust in which the well-being of other people is put in your care during most of their working hours."

— JAMES AUTRY, BESTSELLING AUTHOR AND
FORMER FORTUNE 500 EXECUTIVE

WHY SHOULD WE CONCERN OURSELVES WITH CULTURE IN A conversation about People Economics? The answer is both simple and hard. On the simple side, it matters because it makes a material difference to organizations. Take, for instance, Paul Zack's research at Claremont McKenna College. He found employees in high-trust businesses are 76% more engaged at work and 50% more productive, and 60% enjoyed their jobs more than employees whose firms were in the bottom quartile of measures for trust. He also found employees in high-trust workplaces were 50% more likely to remain in their jobs for the following year.[76]

In addition, trust is an important precursor to employee engagement, and research indicates that high levels of employee engagement translate directly to value creation. A 2016 Willis Towers Watson survey reported "[c]ompanies with high sustainable engagement in their workforce outperform their sector averages for one-year growth in gross profit by 5%; conversely, companies with low sustainable engagement underperform their sectors on one-year profitability growth by 13%."[77]

On the hard side, the Coalition for Inclusive Capitalism's EPIC report says there is "no single, widely accepted definition of what culture is," making it difficult to measure. Yet, they report that "… organizational culture, and its alignment with a company's stated purpose[,] is now a subject of broad investor focus. Increasingly, investors expect companies to be able to explain how boards are monitoring culture, and the course-correcting activity they take when undesirable behaviors and cultural attributes are identified. Companies' cultures are defined by the unique blend of attributes and behaviors people experience when at work."[78]

To address the issue of definition, I suggest we reach back to academic tradition and adopt Edgar Schein's definition of organizational culture. Schein argues:

> … organizational culture can be seen in the assumptions a person makes about the group(s) in which they participate. These assumptions making up culture are grouped into three levels, each level becoming more difficult to articulate and change. These assumptions can be seen through:
>
> 1) artifacts (what you experience with your senses, such as language, styles, stories, and published statements); 2) espoused beliefs and values (ideals, goals and aspirations); and 3) basic underlying beliefs (taken for granted conditions). These assumptions are evident in systems attributes and artifacts, such as:
>
> - Mission, strategy and goals: Why are we all here in this organization? What are we collectively trying to achieve? Do we even know?
>
> - Goals derived from mission: What goals do we set as part of trying to realize that mission? Do we stick to those goals? How are they defined?
>
> - Measuring results and correction mechanisms: How will we know if we achieve those goals? How do we measure it?

- *Remedial and repair strategies: What do we do if something breaks or does not go as planned? Do we have a plan, or do we react?*

- *Means to achieve goals (structure, systems, processes): How do we go about realizing our goals? Do we have systems and procedures in place, or do we trade on strength of personality?* [79]

I will add an additional element to Schein's definition, "purpose" or as Simon Sinek calls it, a "just cause." Sinek defines a just cause as "what inspires us to want to keep playing — leaders who want us to join them in their infinite pursuit must offer us, in clear terms, an affirmative and tangible vision of the ideal future state they imagine."[80] Some may argue that purpose is already included in Schein's model without being identified as an individual element; however, compelling research about the economic value of purpose exists and therefore deserves attention.

Raj Sisiodia, Jagdeth Sheth and David Wolfe in their book *Firms of Endearment* describe a Firm of Endearment (FoE) as a company that *endears* itself to stakeholders by bringing the interests of all stakeholder groups into strategic alignment.[81] They specify that no stakeholder group benefits at the expense of any other stakeholder group. FoE cultures are marked by specific characteristics, among them:

- They subscribe to a purpose for being that is different from and goes beyond making money.

- They actively *align* the interests of all stakeholder groups, not just balance them.

- They operate at the executive level with an open-door policy.

- They consciously humanize the company experience for customers and employees, as well as create a nurturing environment.

- They consider their corporate culture to be their greatest asset and primary source of competitive advantage.

- Their cultures are resistant to short-term, incidental pressures, but also prove able to adapt quickly when needed.

The authors studied a group of 28 FoEs, 18 of which were publicly traded and all of which "best manifested a high standard of humanistic performance." They conducted an investor analysis on the publicly traded firms that revealed FoEs significantly outperformed the S&P 500 over 10-, five- and three-year horizons. Their study showed public FoEs returned 1,026 percent for investors over the 10 years ending June 30, 2006, compared to 122 percent for the S&P 500. That is a more than 8-to-1 ratio.

Intentional cultures are marked by obvious artifacts such as prominent mission or purpose statements; clearly articulated employee value propositions; internal operating structures such as policies, procedures and documented processes; and the like. Unintentional cultures tend to feel less formal or codified but may be just as obvious or identifiable, and even more embedded. Either way, culture has an enormous impact on people and organizations for, as Sisodia and Sheth said, "Employees either benefit or burden every dimension of a company's existence. The extent to which they deliver one or the other is primarily a function of a company culture and leadership's view of employees' value to the company."

THE LINK BETWEEN CULTURE AND EQUITY PERFORMANCE

Can data and data science be used to link culture, human capital and equity performance? A 2020 study, jointly produced by Energage® and Irrational Capital through their research collaboration, shows a credible linkage between corporate culture and equity performance. Looking at stock market performance during the COVID-19 pandemic, they evaluated how culture drives returns. The study included 1,400 public companies recognized as Top Workplaces as determined by their employee engagement scores against Energage's reference benchmarks. Analyzing 10 years of data, 80 million data points, 2.7 million employees and the companies' daily stock returns, Irrational Capital created portfolios of these top workplaces and concluded that "culture driver" portfolios outperformed the S&P 500. The study also looked at what drives Return on Culture (ROC), a metric indicating productivity as a function of stock market performance. They looked to see which companies were more profitable and why, and the link between how people felt about the company and its performance. The study concluded: "It's really easy to beat the S&P 500. To do so, you need to ask employees questions and understand what is going on in the company."[82]

Specifically, this research sought to understand which culture drivers mattered the most during the pandemic. The top three drivers, in order of importance were:

- **People managers who care, help and appreciate.** This was the number-one driver of performance, accounting for more than 10% higher returns for Top Workplace companies over the S&P 500 during the period March through September 2020. Managers helped employees learn and grow, demonstrated their appreciation, and visibly cared about employees' concerns.

- **Inclusive innovation**. This means being open to new and diverse ideas, continuously looking for opportunities for improvement from employees. As a function of openness and flexibility, organizations must ensure all employees have a voice and are being heard, as well as provide autonomy and a sense of individual control. This also means accelerating new ideas and innovation, and putting these ideas into practice. The enemy of this practice is indifference and perceived punishment for trying something new. Inclusion is evident in both the number of ideas and the continuously improving quality of ideas.

- **Is the company moving in the right direction?** Direction was seen as critically important during a period when so much is unknown. Employees needed to feel they were all working toward something. Employee buy-in to the mission of the company was viewed as especially important when employees were not physically co-located and were struggling with increased stress and distraction.

The data showed an increase in caring has a substantial tangible improvement on an organization's economic performance during a crisis. During the first six months of the 2020 pandemic, Top Workplaces did not lose as much value as compared to other S&P 500 companies and outperformed the S&P 500 by three times during their initial recovery.

According to Dan Ariely, co-founder and partner at Irrational Capital:

The results point to the value of recognizing that a person is more than their function at work. Demonstrating that as your manager, I care about you as a person and we understand each other's needs — creating a reciprocal relationship in a dynamic, evolving way. That I want you to develop, improve and grow. I have an interest in your future. People don't recognize the value of appreciation. Saying, 'Thank you.' In an Intel study we conducted[,] we found that compliments from a manager or boss, even via email, generated higher returns and contributed to greater long-term value than spot bonuses or gifts. To put this into context, in this Intel study, saying 'Thank you,' compared to not saying thank you increased production performance in one manufacturing facility by 6%. That's a big deal![83]

When asked if the 2020 study's findings could be extrapolated to private companies, Ariely said his organization had created a dependent measure for the study: stock market performance. Doug Claffey, founder of

Energage, added, "If you think of corporate environments as a machine, there are forces that increase productivity and forces that decrease productivity. The same forces that influence stock market performance in big or public companies apply to similar measures of performance in small or private companies. The distribution of effects in private and small companies is even greater than in large or public companies."[84]

STANDARDIZATION AND CULTURE

In assessing organizational culture, standardization is critical, as is the ability to evaluate an organization period-over-period. Unlike the WEF/IBC Sustainability Metrics framework, the EPIC reporting framework argues that organizations should provide some level of measurement and standardized disclosure about organizational culture, if only in narrative form. They believe standardization will "enable greater comparability across companies and sectors; lend significant credibility to an accompanying narrative report; and ... create data points against which potentially highly meaningful correlations to other relevant business metrics can be identified."[85] The EPIC reporting framework includes a recommended set of standardized survey questions, which they strongly discourage modifying.

I will use work and language already existing in the HR lexicon as a counterpoint to the EPIC framework. This is to illustrate that decades of capturing knowledge and building expertise led by HR already exists. Rather than reinvent the wheel, partnerships with long-established organizations that continue to research and refine measures of trust and employee engagement would be well-advised. Among the many benefits of doing so is the ability to tap into longitudinal data and robust benchmarks that could be used for retrospective analysis and built upon for modeling purposes, as well as enlarged through new technologies being used similarly in sentiment analysis, such as natural language processing (NLP). For this comparison, I will draw on the work of Energage, however, there are other well-known, highly reputable organizations in employee engagement.

EPIC Framework		Energage: What Matters Most at Top Workplaces	
Cultural Dimension	*Standardized Survey Questions*	*Cultural Dimension*	*Standardized Survey Questions* *(sample questions — for a complete list of questions, contact Energage directly)*
Ethics and Integrity	I feel encouraged and supported to speak up. I feel conflicted between doing the right thing for our external stakeholders and performing to meet business expectations.	The Basics	
Alignment with purpose and values	I feel there is a common understanding of our purpose as an organization. It is clear to me how my work contributes to our stated purpose.	OrgHealth™ Alignment	I believe [this company] is going in the right direction.
Leading by example	Based on my experience, leadership consistently demonstrates the organization's stated values in their everyday behavior Based on my experience, leadership engages with the workforce about our culture and values in a meaningful way.	OrgHealth™ Effectiveness	

Performance and accountability	I am clear on what is expected of me from a performance perspective.	OrgHealth™ My Manager	
	I receive timely feedback that strengthens my performance		
Inclusion and well-being	I feel that I have an appropriate work/life balance.	OrgHealth™ Connection	
	I feel supported in developing my long-term career.		
		The Leader	I have confidence in the leader of [this company].
		Engagement	I would highly recommend working at [this company] to others.

You may be asking what was missing from the EPIC framework that made the comparison to Energage's work so important. In my opinion, the biggest (although not the only) gap is in focusing on leadership and management. You may be familiar with the adage "people don't leave companies; they leave managers." In my own career, I have stayed in roles I loathed because I loved my boss, and I have quit companies I adored because my manager couldn't be trusted. Our experience of work is colored by the people we work with and for. It is also heavily influenced by the tone at the top of an organization.

My own doctoral research findings very clearly highlighted the differential impact of CEOs and their executive leadership teams on the culture and climate of an organization.[86] Humanistic leaders create environments of caring, equity, inclusiveness, trust, growth and opportunity for advancement. Their counterparts can create environments of competition, bullying, homogeneity in work groups, micromanaging and poor productivity. This is not new news, and we are finally looking for and finding tangible evidence of value to all stakeholders for high-quality, engaging and inspiring cultures, particularly those that connect organizational efforts with causes larger than themselves.

INTEGRATED THINKING AND ORGANIZATIONAL CULTURE

Impacts and implications for organizational culture extend well beyond the employment experience and return to our earlier concept of integrated thinking. Take, for example, the high-end retailer Nordstrom. One specific aspect of their organizational culture is distributed decision-making and autonomy so associates are empowered to make real-time decisions to delight customers. There are stories of Nordstrom associates accepting returns of items the retailer does not even sell to produce extremely high levels of customer satisfaction. In turn, customers come back to Nordstrom again and again, employees remain with the organization for years, and candidates seek out Nordstrom for employment in a notoriously high-churn environment. In short, high-performing cultures have positive multi-stakeholder impacts, including what the EPIC framework refers to as consumer trust.

In building the EPIC framework, the working group identified and tested five key factors associated with consumer trust and then tested multiple methods for evaluating it. They concluded the "net trust score" was positively correlated to financial performance. The five dimensions of consumer trust in their model are fulfillment of commitment, benevolence of intention, knowledge and skill, truthfulness, and sincerity. While the group recommended using NLP consumer sentiment analysis to evaluate this measure, in the absence of high levels of data sophistication, any organization can use a well-constructed survey and customer retention data to assess its own net promoter score (NPS) as a proxy measure. Although not strictly a human capital component, you can easily see how culture and employees' behaviors attributable to company culture directly translate to consumer trust and financial performance.

This argument makes culture a significant material item for investors. For more than 30 years, study after study has concluded that between 70 and 90 percent of mergers and acquisitions fail to meet important measures of success due to talent and culture issues. In fact, a recent Mercer study looking at people risks in mergers and acquisitions reported that "culture was identified as the number one HR integration challenge."[87]

My own post-acquisition integration work is often colored by issues of culture. For example, a prospective buyer will share how much alike they believe their own organization is to the intended acquisition target. They will cite the similarities in mission and values, and point to the prominent use of the words respect and integrity in both companies' employee value statements. What is often missed is the deeper meaning of each term — the definitions or word-meanings-in-use and behavioral expectations around each value. These are unique to every organization.

For example, ABC Company may recognize respect as fair and equitable pay for all employees and to demonstrate this, publishes employee pay as part of their open-book management philosophy. XYZ Company, which intends to acquire ABC, expects employees to show respect through maintaining formal communication flows; demonstrating deference for higher-ups in a very hierarchical structure; and keeping strict confidences about pay, promotions and benefits. What do you think the first few months post-closing will look and feel like? How much potential value is at stake in these situations?

THE HIGH COST OF EMPLOYEE TURNOVER

In 2019 alone, voluntary turnover costs exceeded $630 billion USD. The Work Institute's 2020 Retention Report said 78% of the reasons employees quit were preventable by the employer.[88] Their data showed career development as the number-one reason for voluntary turnover, followed by work-life balance and manager behavior. Frustration and yearning are evident in the voices of the Work Institute's survey participants:

- *I didn't feel like there was any more room for me to grow, I was there over 4 years and I did not receive a raise.*

- *There is very little room for growth opportunities. People with disabilities, such as myself, are not considered for opportunities.*

- *A promotion opportunity was available, and someone was hired with dramatically less experience than me.*

- *I left the company because the job description did not match what I wound up doing, it was not a good fit for me.*

- *I left the company because the schedule was not working for my kids and my family. I was working 12 hours a day.*

- *I was being harassed and bullied by my supervisors.*

- *I left because of a conflict with my direct manager. She treated blacks and whites differently, and also treated patients poorly. I tried to get to talk with someone in HR, but they kept blowing me off.*

We can't always know what keeps people engaged and happy in their roles, but we come much closer to understanding what makes our employees productive when we hear their voices directly. In a recent SOCAP Global panel discussion, Brian McGannon of the Forum for Sustainable and Responsible Investment (US SIF) argued that employee engagement and value creation rest on "looking at the lowest tier of employees." You never know what someone's employment experience truly is until you ask the questions. To illustrate this point, listen to the voice of an actual employee through an excerpt of her exit interview. (To maintain her privacy, we will call her Ellie.)

Ellie was a strong performer and valued member of her team. She had worked in the pressing department for more than a year when she came to her supervisor to give notice of her resignation. Ellie's supervisor asked why she was leaving, to which she replied:

> *Your job wasn't bad. In the short time I've worked here, I noticed that some people don't like being moved. I moved to someone else's spot and that person was unhappy, and it made the other team members unhappy, too. If you don't need to move people, then don't. It would be nice to ask them before you make changes, because when you don't, you can feel their dislike all around you. Also, your time clock is a computer and takes too long to clock in and out. If everyone is getting paid the same, you shouldn't need to input all those codes just for hourly pay.*
>
> *Something in the steam causes my fingertips, hands, back and head to ache to the touch; maybe I have an allergy to the soap? Plus, the steam smells like drugs and like men and women who had sex. By the way, you come home with that smell on you!*

LISTEN

Listening is a critically important element of positive culture-building and a necessary component of thriving, high-performing work groups and individuals. We need to feel heard, acknowledged and appreciated to do our best work. Perhaps Ellie would have stayed had her supervisor asked about her work experiences and addressed her concerns before she took another job. During periods of uncertainty, listening and being heard are even more critical. According to Energage and Irrational Capital, managers should ask the following questions as a litmus test to gauge employee engagement and to ensure economic performance at all times, especially during times of instability:

1. How are you doing? How can I help?

2. What can we do differently to do better?

3. Where are we headed — and why?

And, use the most powerful two words, "Thank you."[89]

CHAPTER 7

The Impact of Leaders

"What a man sees depends both upon what he looks at and also upon what his previous visual-conceptual experience has taught him to see."

— THOMAS KUHN, PHYSICIST, HISTORIAN
AND PHILOSOPHER OF SCIENCE

THOMAS KUHN SAID THAT A PARADIGM IS THE ENTIRE constellation of beliefs, values and techniques shared by the members of a given community that denote the solutions they employ. He said further that a paradigm governs not a subject matter but rather, a group of practitioners.[90] It stands to reason, then, that a paradigm shift requires reframing the beliefs, values, language and world views of those who are members of a would-be new community. In this chapter, we will take a look at paradigms, practitioners and the making of a revolution.

One such practitioner is Amit Mohindra, founder and CEO of People Analytics Success, who believes finance and human resources fundamentally hold opposing worldviews or paradigms. "For example," he argues, "employee vacancies or job openings — finance views these vacancies as positive to the extent that they represent savings in overall costs of labor during the period a position remains unfilled. Human resources see this same vacancy as a risk to performance, productivity, knowledge transfer and more." The lens through which each of these groups of practitioners sees the same issue colors their perspective. "Additionally, there is an uneven power differential in that CEOs are much more likely to be persuaded by the financial perspective, rendering the human resources argument moot."[91]

Who should be held accountable for value creation or depletion as it relates to intangible assets in general and people specifically? Regulators, educators, investors, executives, boards of directors and employees themselves. We all play a part in the value creation framework, although those with much greater influence will undoubtedly alter the course for businesses and their people.

BOARD DIRECTORS

On December 1, 2020, NASDAQ filed a proposal with the SEC to adopt new listing rules related to board diversity and disclosure.[92] If approved by the SEC, the new rules would require all companies listed on Nasdaq's U.S. exchange to publicly disclose consistent and transparent diversity statistics regarding their board of directors. The rules would also require most Nasdaq-listed companies to have, or explain why they do not have, at least two diverse directors, including one who self-identifies as female and one who self-identifies as either an underrepresented minority or LGBTQ+.

As part of the rationale for the new requirements, Nasdaq's proposal presents an analysis of more than two dozen studies that found an association between diverse boards, better financial performance and corporate governance. This is a clear example of the investment marketplace exerting pressure on regulators to influence publicly traded companies and their boards of directors. Despite existing evidence regarding the value of diverse boards, 75% of the Nasdaq-listed companies do not meet the proposed guidelines and as of 2018, 30% of public company boards were still made up exclusively of men. Even among those boards who have greater female representation, the women are predominantly white.

Change at the board level is crucial for People Economics principles to be adopted. Researchers like Laura Morgan Roberts and Anthony Mayo advocate shifting from an exclusive focus on the business case for racial diversity to a moral one that promotes real conversations about race, revamping diversity and inclusion programs, and managing career development better at every stage. As they explain, this will require executives to "think deeply about their ethics and corporate culture and exert extra effort for a cause they may not consider central to their business."[93]

At the board level, a shift of mindsets is necessary to avoid tokenism and ensure stakeholders can reap all the available rewards of inclusive and diverse collaborations. Personally, I advocate thinking even more broadly about diversity and inclusion to gain richer and more-comprehensive perspectives. This means selecting those who are differently able and possess skills, abilities, points of view, experiences and traits that go beyond surface-level qualities.

CHIEF EXECUTIVE OFFICER

Google returns 350 million items when you search for the definition of CEO. Clearly, these are not all unique definitions, but it is safe to say every person reading this book will have a view about the role and responsibilities of a chief executive officer. For the purposes of this discussion, I will expand the title to include founder, president or executive director — the highest-ranking individual in an organization with responsibility for managerial decision-making. To further refine the topic, I would like to focus on the CEO's responsibilities with respect to implications for human capital and culture.

One of the most-important functions of the chief executive is articulating and reinforcing the organization's purpose; that is, answering the question "Why are we in business?" The answer must be compelling, meaningful, inspiring and long-term–focused. In their Statement on the Purpose of a Corporation, members of the Business Roundtable, a collaborative of premier U.S. business leaders, committed to bringing value to their customers, investing in their employees, dealing fairly and ethically with their suppliers, supporting the communities in which they work, and generating long-term value for shareholders. Their commitment begins with this sentence: "Americans deserve an economy that allows each person to succeed through hard work and creativity and to lead a life of meaning and dignity."[94]

The role of a chief executive is to animate purpose through value creation. The CEO has to know where and through what means the organization creates value and how to foster an environment designed for value acceleration. An inventory of the organization's historical strengths and capabilities will be particularly helpful and can be accomplished through insights gleaned from all stakeholders. Once captured, the capabilities can be used as tools for reimagining and reinvention. I recommend this as a perpetual exercise, similar to adopting a continuous improvement methodology. Constant practice will enable nimble responses, adaptation, evolution and the occasional pivot. When consistently checked against the organization's purpose, the findings connect prioritization, investment, strategic and tactical decision-making to every aspect of business operation.

As paradigms about leaders and organizations shift, there are other trends to consider. Chief executives and their teams will be tasked with navigating turbulence at a minimum, and perhaps even more of the chaos we recently experienced. According to studies by organizations such as IBM and McKinsey, for organizations to thrive, they must be capable of faster decision-making with imperfect information; move away from bureaucratic hierarchies to create flatter and more-flexible structures; support rapid redeployment of talent for critical needs, innovation and creative solutioning; and become expert collaborators and partners within and outside the organization. They both point to talent and culture as prerequisites for long-term success.[95] [96]

An intentional and positive culture includes building trust; championing transparency, fairness and equity; empowering others through ownership, inclusivity, autonomy and collaborative decision-making; balancing supportive and challenging leadership styles and taking calibrated risks.

Talent has to be treated as your scarcest resource. That means CEOs will understand that other company assets like technology, access to raw materials, intellectual property and customer relationships are not the true sustainable advantage; rather, it is the ability to harness the passion, skills, capabilities, judgment and creativity that people bring to work. Doing this well requires proficiency and discernment.

Success in any role is context-dependent. CEOs can model exemplary talent management by understanding and articulating which roles in the organization are most important, and how these roles contribute to value creation and purpose; carefully and collaboratively crafting the criteria for success; evaluating and developing candidates fairly and equitably against these criteria; and empowering others in the organization to participate in the process.

Add to this list, adopting a new view of the economic calculus governing definitions of business success. This requires a significant transformation in accounting and measuring organization outputs, prioritization of investments and expectations for value creation. By necessity, this also changes the roles, functions and capabilities of the constellation of leaders at the top of an organization — beginning with the CFO.

CHIEF FINANCIAL OFFICER

Larry Fink, American billionaire business leader and chair and CEO of BlackRock, wrote in a 2020 letter to CEOs: "Awareness is rapidly changing, and I believe we are on the edge of a fundamental reshaping of finance." This single line has been repeated and reported on by academics, journalists, political pundits and investors. What is even more compelling is the final sentence in the section of this letter, which focused on improved disclosure for shareholders: "Given the groundwork we have already laid [about] engaging on disclosure, and the growing investment risks surrounding sustainability, we will be increasingly disposed to vote against management and board directors when companies are not making sufficient progress on sustainability-related disclosures and the business practices and plans underlying them." [97]

If you ask why this matters, consider that BlackRock is the world's largest asset manager, with $8.67 trillion in assets under management (AUM) as of January 2021. Most of the money BlackRock invests is in retirement funds for individuals and pension holders like frontline workers, teachers and businesspeople. They have enormous power and influence in the marketplace and on the practices of the businesses and leaders they invest in. If Larry Fink says finance will be reshaped, then the world listens — especially CFOs.

During the summer of 2020, the CEOs of IFAC, IIRC and AICPA co-authored a white paper where they reframed the role of CFOs and finance professionals in organizational value creation:

> … Many chief financial officers (CFOs) are caught in an old paradigm in which financial information and returns to shareholders are the primary measure of performance and success. A short-term capital markets mindset often results in narrow measures of value creation. Broader information on value creation covering critical assets such as people, innovation, data and key relationships; environmental, social and governance (ESG) factors; and wider impacts, [is] needed to serve all key stakeholders better and more sustainably. [98]

Practically, such changing expectations will require CFOs and their finance colleagues to take on the role of trusted advisor and partner to the business, using employee, customer, financial and operational data to improve customer and employee experiences. They will be called upon to interpret customer needs and translate them into value creation opportunities. CFOs will be looked to as architects for change — influencers who must adopt a holistic view of the enterprise, implement technology and use data wisely. These responsibilities include establishing clear links between financial and non-financial metrics; identifying the activities and initiatives needed among human, social, relationship and other relevant capitals and resources to drive financial value; ensuring operating margins; conducting root-cause analysis; and identifying value leakage. Some are suggesting finance should take ultimate responsibility for ESG performance in their organizations.

CHIEF PEOPLE OFFICER

Also referred to as the Chief Human Resources Officer (CHRO), the Chief People Officer (CPO) is the top-level manager or executive in charge of a company's workforce. In a January 2020 study released by the Executive Network of the Society for Human Resources (SHRM) , two organizations — HR People + Strategy (HRPS) and Willis Towers Watson — defined the role the CPO as "to imagine, invent and ignite the change that will ensure the ongoing relevance of its talent and forward-looking work strategies essential to an organization's future business success."[99] This survey points to CPOs as the change agent, advancing organizational agility and preparing businesses for perpetually shifting environments. Compliance and operations are merely table stakes.

Despite the importance of this function, only a third of those surveyed, including CEOs, board members, executive peers and CPOs themselves, believe future CPOs are getting the skills development necessary to excel in the future. These skills include "embracing technology that builds a consumer experience for employees; moving from episodic training to perpetual reskilling; and leading with data-driven insights." The survey respondents also viewed CPOs and CEOs collectively as the drivers of business achievements coupled with creating "inclusive, innovative and productive work ecosystems."

HRPS and Willis Towers Watson made compelling arguments for the adoption of technology to augment and improve performance levels; improve recruitment and retention; and support real-time and on-demand learning, re-skilling and knowledge transfer. "CPOs need to have the digital business acumen necessary to evaluate new technologies and ... understand work and how technical skills fit into the organization, ... how changing technology can impact the workforce." This knowledge and expertise are essential, especially in technology-driven, virtual work environments.

The final recommendation of the HRPS + Willis Towers Watson CPO study was to elevate decision science and analytics to promote people-centered insights and innovation. Since this survey was conducted, we have seen acceleration of transparency in sustainability metrics and human capital measures, making tech-enabled reporting, disclosure and analytics a requirement, at least for public companies. This, despite IBM's conclusion that fewer than 20% of organizations have the capability to apply predictive analytics to address important people issues.[100]

Charan, Barton and Carey, in their 2015 Article *People Before Strategy: A New Role for the CHRO,* compared the role of the CFO to the role of the CPO. They said a CFO's job is partly defined by the investment community, the board, outside auditors and regulators, while the CPO/CHRO's role is solely defined by the CEO.[101] That is changing dramatically, as evidenced by the shift toward a multi-stakeholder economy replete with emerging reporting requirements and investor demand for greater transparency about human capital practices. Those heading up people practices will be defined as much by external forces as the role of CFO. In fact, stronger relationships between finance, human resources and technology will result from these shifts because measurement, reporting and value creation relies heavily on experts in these disciplines. Paul Washington, executive director of the ESG Center at the Conference Board, argues that it is vitally important to include human resources professionals in crafting 10-K disclosures, because they are the experts and should contribute details, including the human capital narrative.[102]

In truth, the HR function has struggled with credibility for decades, often using the argument that they weren't being granted a seat at the table.

In many organizations, this remains true. Why? Some have attributed it to a lack of knowledge, interest in and expertise about the business; the HR function has been perceived as having little business acumen, imbalanced in favor of the employee, and purely an administrative support or compliance function. We have a long road left to travel.

A stark reminder of the gulf between HR as an apex value creator and the current importance CEOs attribute to the function is clear in the IBM Institute for Business Value's 2021 CEO study, "Find your essential: How to thrive in a post-pandemic reality." The findings reveal CEOs' concerns about the top external forces likely to affect their businesses. Regulatory concerns jumped to second on the list at 50%, and people skills were identified as a solid fifth out of nine factors at 44%. However, when asked to identify which other members of the C-suite are likely to play the most-crucial roles for their organizations, CHROs were dead last at 16%. CFOs, COOs and CIO/CTOs came in at 57%, 56% and 39% respectively.[103]

At no time in modern history have issues of people, value creation, equity, equality, data and decision-making, transparency, reputation, and corporate morality been more intertwined. This is a crucible moment for HR in businesses large and small. Just having a seat at the table is meaningless if you struggle to speak the language once you get there. There is still a chasm to cross. Without a common language and standard frameworks to articulate a cogent case for investment in people and HR-related technology, efforts aimed at diverting dollars away from traditional capital investments will still fall on deaf ears.

INVESTORS

One of the most-powerful quotes I have read about investors — all shapes and sizes — is by Harvard Business School luminaries Michael Porter, George Serafeim and Mark Kramer: "We believe the most fundamental purpose of investors is to allocate capital to those businesses that can use it well in meeting society's most important needs at a profit. Without the effective investment of capital in the real economy, society cannot prosper.

But we live in a world today where investors are profiting while much of society is struggling. This disconnect is a threat not only to the legitimacy of capital markets, but also to the future of capitalism itself."[104]

Institutional investors recognize the shift toward value creation through intangible assets. This dramatic shift drives demand for reporting changes to enable insight into various aspects of business operations, according to Aeisha Mastagni, a portfolio manager at CalSTRS, one of the largest and most-influential institutional investors in the U.S. In a panel discussion conducted by the Conference Board, Mastagni argued for human capital as a competitive advantage for businesses, pointing to CalSTRS's "Investment Belief 7"[105] that responsible corporate governance includes the management of ESG factors as a mandate for evaluating human capital measures, such as number of employees (full-time, part-time and contingent), TCOW, and workforce diversity.

According to Mastagni, "We used to focus on boards. Now we look at gender, ethnicity and race at different levels of the organization. We continue to push regulators for human capital standards and metrics, putting our weight behind the SASB standards." That insight into organizations' investments in employee training and development is key to understanding workforce capacity for the future. To that end, proxies can be read to understand the long-term narrative. "They are one of the best places to tell your story — board details, compensation strategies, promotion and succession plans." When asked about the recent SEC human capital disclosure requirements, which mandate additional information in public companies' 10-Ks, Mastagni said "the 10-Ks are mostly of interest to analysts." [106]

I asked my friend and colleague Sarah Kim, an active and experienced investor who was formerly with Halyard Capital, for her thoughts about ESG and human capital practices of general partners and limited partners. I prompted her response with this quote from Judy Samuelson's book *The Six New Rules of Business: Creating Real Value in a Changing World*:

"New Rule: Reputation, trust, and other intangibles drive business value. Trust of employees and business partners, and premium access to talent and natural resources, are the source of real value and cannot be discounted or measured in traditional ways. To understand their value requires breaking down the walls between the health of the business and the health of the business ecosystem."[107]

Here is how Sarah responded:

I am seeing promising trends in the private equity/asset management ecosystem on the social, environmental and human capital front. The scope of investment due diligence, for example, has expanded to include valuation analysis, risk assessments centered on ESG (the extent of which depends on the size, growth phase, industry), extending to supply chain integrity at the portfolio company level and human capital elements (diversity, equity and inclusion — DEI) at both the portfolio company and fund level. Asset managers (GPs and LPs) have started to build dedicated teams to manage the firm's ESG integration efforts throughout the entire investment cycle (and in some cases, they are on the investment committee, which I strongly believe is the right approach), advising and collaborating with deal teams during due diligence with regard to sustainability and socially responsible alignment and orienting to serve all the stakeholders' interest.

As an investor, it is of paramount importance to focus on human and intellectual capital elements, which tend to be in a lower-priority due diligence bucket. I believe that investors should allocate a meaningful number of resources to build and utilize a network of industry thought leaders, C-suite executives and advisors to assess value and risk/return on human capital. I strongly encourage this discipline. It is my philosophy that people — their intellectual capacity, integrity, culture and foresight — are critical factors to success, or causes for failure when absent. It is necessary to perform an in-depth evaluation at the outset when evaluating an investment opportunity as to who and how employees (at least top quartile) have driven growth and how they will contribute to value creation (or cause value leakage). This insight informs us in valuing businesses, structuring trans-actions and aligning interests with management.

While an investor may not explicitly assign value to human/ intellectual capital when arriving at a purchase price, it may be implicitly built into enterprise value through creative structures. Allocation of a portion of sale proceeds at exit to members of the team instrumental in accelerating value creation is just one example. The above distribution, in some cases, can be made ahead of the investors in a distribution waterfall. While this could potentially dilute ROI, it implies that intrinsic value in human/intellectual capital (beyond the traditional financial metrics) was recognized at the entry point. The PE industry has made significant progress. When monetizing investments, value and risks associated ESG, human capital and transparency have become an increasingly important part of the valuation analysis.

In the ESG and sustainability arena, some LPs have been addressing this matter for many years. Certain LPs began requesting that GPs disclose information on the team composi-tion and its diversity profile, including compensation and car-ry-allocation structure by gender and race. It is heartening to see that GPs have begun to heighten their focus on impact, equitable and sustainable drivers. PEs have the opportunity to influence their portfolio companies in implementing social, environment and impact-driven capabilities, including supply chain integrity, diversity and inclusion. PEs, as owners and members of boards of directors, have responsibilities and positions of influence toward this effort and can create and stimulate multiplier effects in society.

While I believe that intangibles, such as reputation, talent, leadership and contribution to society, drive value, consistent measurement throughout the business community and PE industry will require unified effort.

As an investor, I support Judy's "Six New Rules." I strongly believe that reputation, trust and other intangibles are key elements to success as mentioned above. We must evaluate current financial health, future financials and risks by identifying these intangibles and the linkage between them and value of the enterprise which are often derived by multiples of earnings before interest taxes depreciation and amortization (EBITDA) or revenue.

We are at a juncture where it is critical to collaborate with all stakeholders in the ecosystem. A collaborative effort amongst all constituents has already led to meaningful progress in developing paths and metrics to measure and manage our progress. Much more to come ..." [108]

Sarah's perspectives echo my own experiences working with investors and strategic acquirers. It is not unusual to work with a first-time private equity client who has limited their human capital due diligence process to matters of health and welfare benefits, retirement savings and outstanding legal claims alone. While these are important investment considerations, they barely scratch the surface of risk and compliance-related items. They do not provide insight into the essence of value contributed (or lost) through people and related processes or practices.

CHAPTER 8

Requisites for a Renaissance

"The purpose of a company is to engage all its stakeholders
in shared and sustained value creation."

— KLAUS SCHWAB, CHAIR, WORLD ECONOMIC FORUM,
DAVOS MANIFESTO 2020

WRITING THIS BOOK HAS BEEN AN EXERCISE IN MEANING-MAKING and puzzle-solving. An added benefit has been enlarging my thinking and hearing other's views and perspectives. I am still working through the implications of a perspective shared by my academic colleague John Dumay at Macquarie University. I asked him what had to change in corporate accounting practices to improve recognition of value creation and investment in intangible assets. His response, after he asked if I really wanted his opinion, was, "Who cares?"

"Who cares?" I thought. "*I* care! Of course, I care; isn't that why I embarked on this adventure in the first place?" Rather than respond with righteous indignation, I asked a slew of additional questions and took some time to ponder his replies.

Here is one provocative view. Perhaps we are better served by looking at accounting practices as a set of tools designed to help inform decision-making and tell one part of the story of business. In the context of a building project, for example, one useful tool would be a budget, which provides decision-making parameters, guidelines and measures of success. If you were building a house, the budget would be just one, albeit an important, factor in your project management, but you wouldn't look to your spreadsheet to decide where your windows should go. You would look to a set of user-requirements first: how many people will live in the house, where will it be built, the view you'd like to have, and any special needs or desires to be considered. Designs and blueprints would be created and carefully followed to ensure the integrity and acceptable outcomes of the project; these are a corollary to the underpinning purpose, philosophies, guiding principles and values of an organization. So I ask: *Are we living in a house designed using a budget rather than a blueprint?*

Lady Lynn Forester DeRothschild, founder of the Coalition for Inclusive Capitalism, has said, "This is no time to be quiet. Equality and inclusiveness is of primary concern for workers and we need partnership from government to assist. The investment community has to prove they mean what they've said, and it will require pain for those who have benefited from these policies in the past."[109]

Evolution requires we learn from history and embrace our experiences keeping the parts that continue to contribute to engaged workforces, thriving employees and strong organizations. We need to cast away a singular focus on profits and shareholder wealth creation in exchange for more holism, equity, equality and inclusive capitalism. What follows are my thoughts about what might pave the way for such a renaissance and some of the requisites for renewal.

INTEGRATED THINKING REVISITED

In his book *The Opposable Mind*, Roger Martin describes integrated thinking as "the predisposition and the capacity to hold two diametrically opposed ideas in one's head. And then, without panicking or settling for one alternative or the other[,] produce a synthesis that is superior to either opposing idea."[110]

While this capability may not come naturally to some, I argue it is a skill and habit worth developing. A way to build this habit is to practice saying, "Yes, and ...," which is the hallmark quality of improvisational comedy. In this process, you replace the word "but" with "and," which allows you to invite additional thoughts, ideas and suggestions — promoting positive interactions and improving brainstorming, for one. Applying a "Yes, and …" approach to problem-solving and decision-making opens the door to idea generation and developing synergies.

Here is a brief example of how this might work. It is mid-October, and you are in the final throes of budgeting for the next fiscal year. You and your peers are reviewing the most-recent budget and you have to shave $10k for final approval. As the conversation flows around the table, each person responds with, "Yes, we know that funds are tight, but …" Your CTO says she needs to invest in technology upgrades for half the team, and your CMO says he's already committed to the rebranding contract with an outside design firm, and you have offers for three new employees already in place … and so it goes.

The final person at the table is your head of R&D. She pipes up and asks if anyone followed up on the inquiry she received from another firm to use the company's lab capability as a contract research partner. She had shared a preliminary estimate of the work to be done and her staff and facilities capabilities with the CFO and general counsel. At prevailing industry rates, she argues, her team could take on the work and earn more than double the existing budget shortfall in Q1 alone. Doing so would also be a pilot for offering this and other services more broadly in the future. She approached the budget constraints with a "Yes, and …" perspective, solved the current budget issues and opened the door to greater opportunities for the future.

OUTWARD MINDSET

No book or article on leadership in the 21st century is complete without reference to emotional intelligence (EQ) or empathy. It is the currency of trust. Being able to walk a mile in someone else's shoes, to listen attentively and to have compassion for their situation is the connective tissue for meaningful relationships and belonging. This is not a new concept. Adam

Smith's *Theory of Moral Sentiments* was written to remind us all that empathy is our principal responsibility in business and society.

Empathy requires what the Arbinger Institute calls an "outward mindset." A mindset is our unique way of seeing the world and others in it. Taken positively, mindsets help us process information, make sense of our world and enhance our speed to decision-making. However, mindsets may also reinforce biases and stereotypes, limit our ability to see alternative points of view, or discount critical information. As the Arbinger Institute explains: "With an outward mindset, I am alive to and interested in others' needs, objectives and challenges; I see others as people. With an inward mindset, on the other hand, I become self-focused and see others not as people with their own needs, objectives and challenges but as objects that help me with mine. Those that can help me, I see as vehicles. Those that make things more difficult for me, I see as obstacles. Those whose help wouldn't matter become irrelevant to me."[111]

Organizational value is created through positive employee, customer, user, patient, participant and other stakeholder experiences. Without the critical ability to see and feel these other perspectives (an outward mindset), it is easy to lose focus on our business purpose, mission and intended ways of being. Inclusivity and empathy are hallmarks of strong business and societal cultures, connected communities, deep interpersonal relationships and brands consumers love. Like consistent contributions to a piggy bank, investing in a strong outward mindset is change you can bank on.

RENEW THE FINANCE FUNCTION

At a tactical level, an important aspect of financial renewal will be movement toward standardized accounting frameworks. Proponents of this evolution suggest the U.S. move away from GAAP standards and adopt the IFRS standards to ensure comparability and common terminology for U.S. and ex-U.S. accounting practices. Beyond this lies a cry for change of a different nature. As IFAC and AICPA argue:

The enhanced role that the CFO and finance function can play in accounting for value creation will result in a stronger and more effective finance and accounting profession that sits at the heart of organizations. Both integrated thinking and reporting, as well as impact measurement and management, are becoming more mainstream. This area is of particular importance for understanding, measuring and providing confidence in business performance, and involves accountants working closely with others from a wide range of disciplines and perspectives.[112]

Money equals power, influence and control. Adages such as "capital is king" persist for a reason, perhaps in the hope they will continue as self-fulfilling prophecies. Nonetheless, many businesses experience value creation and profitability through intangibles alone; the currency of their future logs in at the beginning of the day and logs out in the evening. Customer relationships rest squarely on employee interactions and innovation derives from the creativity inspired by internal climate, management style and compelling purpose — the worker's experience. The finance function has enjoyed a privileged and powerful position in most organizations. Our future rests on greater collaboration, shared power and control, and a systems-wide view of value creation.

A NEW PEOPLE PARADIGM

"Our employees are our most important asset." How many times have you seen this in advertising, corporate communications and employee handbooks? Imagine for a moment that employees were diamonds. They would be carefully faceted for brilliance and shine, polished and cleaned to show great luster, zealously guarded for safekeeping, and displayed with pride under the best lighting and on beautiful velvet trays. Their value would be measured in carat-weight and described to onlookers and would-be buyers using terms that described their intrinsic properties: "It will make your sweetheart swoon. Won't you be proud to see it on her finger?" as well as their extrinsic properties — crystal-clear, flawless and will hold its value forever. Only the most-trustworthy and capable caretakers would have access to the diamonds, and the diamonds would only ever leave your possession in exchange for something even more valuable, or perhaps not at all.

Why is it then that the care and keeping of employees (remember, these are a company's most-important asset, like diamonds) is met with frustration and ridicule from business leaders? Our current business models favor financial and material assets at the expense of human capital. As Bruno Roche and Jay Jakub wrote in *Completing Capitalism: Heal Business to Heal the World:* "Simply skewing the balance in favor of one category of capital at the expense of others is counterproductive over time. To do so is a proverbial 'half-truth' (a lie), albeit a seductive one. It is only when all pillars of prosperity are balanced — in terms of account[ing] for what each pillar contributes to the system and how each pillar is remunerated — will prosperity be lasting."[113]

I recently asked a colleague about this and her reply was, "Business leaders get the HR capabilities they deserve." That is to say, if the function is perceived as an administrative burden or worse, a necessary evil rather than a value-creating partner in a firm, it will attract and retain those with limited human resources interest and talent. My fear is even the most positively intended regulatory changes and disclosure requirements will render HR a compliance function, subsumed under finance or risk management, because the value of people is still unrecognized and continues to be discounted. The antidote is a paradigm change.

All other assets in a business are invested in, rendering them more valuable. Invest in the talent, enabling structures and technologies that cultivate your greatest asset. Make HR more valuable, and you have enriched your entire organization.

Those of you who are in HR have both opportunity and accountability. You must invest in yourselves and your function. Learn the language of business. Develop collaborative relationships with your peers in other critical functions, such as finance, investor relations, legal affairs, operations, technology and communications. Together, your collaboration can educate and inform about ways to build and measure value throughout the organization. Get curious about the business and the shifting environment, build your technical proficiencies, seek out mentors within and outside your business, and advocate for human capital technology and data analytics. Your long-term success, and professional relevance, depends on it.

DATA AND ANALYTICS

Start small and start now. Take inventory of your current data-gathering capabilities. If you decide to begin your journey by looking at turnover, where will your data come from? Do you have strong data-gathering and reporting capabilities already built into your payroll and time-keeping systems, and are you confident that new hire, leaves of absence and termination data are current? If you suspect your recordkeeping processes and data integrity need work, that's a great place to make changes or additions. There is no need to boil the ocean.

Work with what you have and enlist the support and capabilities of others. Approach this as a learning process and even a "game." When my daughter was little, she loved the movie "Harriet the Spy." To keep her interest in activities, we positioned them as spy games. She would learn through finding clues, looking for patterns, exploring cause-and-effect, and asking "why" over and over and over again. Gamifying the data-gathering process is a fun and interesting way to approach your journey.

Look for patterns in your data and ask lots of questions:

- Why do terminations happen most often during the summer months?

- Why is employee retention so high in the quality assurance department and so low in product development?

- How does training spend correspond to voluntary or involuntary turnover in specific departments?

Pick a "metric of the month" and explore it. Do you have reliable data to use for measuring this metric? Does the measurement tell you something interesting, useful and important about the way your organization functions and creates value? Does this measure connect with other organization measures, such as manufacturing performance and productivity, customer satisfaction, and other important KPIs? Look for interesting correlations.

Once you have played with this a bit, look back at your systems and processes to see where you have strengths you can build upon. You may, for example, decide that while your enterprise resources technology is great for basic employment and financial data, it doesn't provide the robust information you would like to see for recruitment and promotion or succession planning purposes.

SUPPORTIVE STRUCTURES

Most organizations are built to be stable, in part because stability is a precursor for short-term success. Stable environments lend themselves to repeatable processes, consistent and high-quality outputs, and speed. In highly volatile environments, these structures lose their competitive advantage. Organization designs and skills built on responsiveness, change agility and with an eye toward constant evolution are much more likely to weather turbulent times.

(The term "organization" can be used to describe not only companies, but also institutions, governments, foundations, schools, churches and so on.)

In their book *Built to Change*, Edward Lawler and Christopher Worley describe the requirements for organizations that are built to change: "They must view people as open and willing to learn and as eager to try new things. They must have structures that are constantly refocusing attention and resources on both current and future problems and opportunities. They must have reward systems that encourage learning and growth as well as current value-added activities. Finally, they must have financial processes and other systems that support innovation and the start-up of new products and services."[114]

An example of a change-ready structure is a worker cooperative, where the organization is owned and self-managed by the employees. According to the Democracy at Work Institute, "a worker cooperative is a values-driven business that puts worker and community benefit at the core of its purpose."[115] The principles of a worker cooperative are a) employees own the business and share in its financial success based on their individual contributions, and b) employees are represented on the board of directors, adhering to one employee/worker–one vote principles. Cooperatives may or may not be change-agile, but they are designed to be egalitarian and because they are community-focused, they tend to be more responsive to shifts in the environment.

A relatively new entrant to the organization structure stage is the benefit corporation, sometimes referred to as public benefit corporation. Certified B Corporations balance purpose and profit. They are legally required to consider the impact of their decisions on their workers, customers, suppliers, community and the environment. Many organizations you are familiar with are certified B Corps and have committed to meeting very high standards of social and environmental, transparency and accountability performance. These are public and private, for-profit and not-for-profit organizations that have volunteered to "use business as a force for good."[116]

NEW DIRECTIONS FOR DIRECTORS

Positive change requires real courage on the part of boards of directors. Simply disclosing more information about organizations they represent is not the answer. They need to move beyond legacy ways of doing things and align with the health of these enterprises. Diversifying boards is an important first step. Adding women, people of color and LGBTQ+ members is essential. More importantly, these measures have to capture the voices, experience and expertise of these members. Tokenism must not be allowed.

Directors must champion the use of data and analytics in board-level decision-making, as well as invite members of the enterprise with line-of-sight to the impact and implications of the data to share their insights and answer board-member questions. They should tie these data to CEO and executive compensation structures, moving away from stock returns as the sole or primary index of performance and instead look toward annualized measures of management, culture, employee well-being and safety, and long-term measures of value creatio and returns.

Cultural concerns are often considered a third-rail issue and have been difficult for boards to address, but the climate contributing to a thriving workforce is a significant consideration for workers and investors alike. As the demand for transparency continues to increase, boards ought to seek opportunities to communicate with various stakeholders about executive pay, job structures, equity and opportunity, and succession.

PARTNERS FOR PROGRESS

We are at the very early stages of what is likely to be a long journey. Success will require coordinated effort and many hands. Governments, investors, business leaders, policy and practice framers, educators, employees, consumers, and others all have a part to play. Today we are seeing regulatory changes focused on measurement and disclosure of material information in publicly traded organizations. Where does this leave workers in private businesses, nonprofits and government agencies, should their employers also have some requirements for disclosure?

Regulators and policymakers must be vigilant and careful in the creation of standards and regulations, taking a realistic, context-sensitive approach and remembering that rules often change because some try to take advantage for their own benefit. Regulators must adjust for when this happens and respond reasonably to public demands for change, while bearing in mind the potential for unintended consequences when doing the right thing.

Investors (LPs, GPs and individual investors) must stand behind organizations who are committed to making a difference. Businesses large and small are committed to multi-stakeholder economies and are making strides toward voluntary disclosure often connected to their purpose, mission and values; these efforts must be recognized and rewarded. Framers, advisors and professional associations can come together to create common language, standardize where appropriate, and provide direction and counsel when flexible approaches could be most beneficial. These groups can nurture collaboration, capture constituent voices and needs, drive related changes in business school curricula and professional education, and lead efforts toward progress.

EDUCATION

In *The Six New Rules of Business,* Judy Samuelson writes: "Teachers and scholars in management schools are insulated from the pace and chaos of markets and business decision-making. The tension between theory and practice can be a healthy one. The principal ideas and analytical frameworks that are taught in finance classrooms — and shape the attitude and frameworks in professional domains like consulting and finance — may lag behind what's current today, the thinking goes, but they stand the test of time."[117]

We can't afford the lag, and the test of time has merely proven that principles can fail us. We are creatures of habit and prefer stability, so we double-down on what we think we know. Change is difficult and messy; intangibles are hard to measure; and no one wants to be wrong. It is time to flip the script and adopt an agile mindset for thinking about education. According to McKinsey & Company, agile methodologies include "the ability to quickly reconfigure strategy, structure, processes, people, and technology toward value-creating and value-protecting opportunities."[118]

There is a strong call for public-private partnership in addressing issues of social and racial injustice, and shifting toward a multi-stakeholder economy. Wouldn't our educational institutions and their students benefit from a similar model? In partnership with companies, investors, consumers and others, educators would be able to tap into the rapid changes, perhaps even prognosticate evolution or as contemporary business leaders say, "see around the corners." Such collaboration enables current and future stakeholders to adopt a systems-wide perspective and understand value creation and measurement from a whole new vantage point, while developing skills in integrated thinking, boundary-spanning and collaborative problem-solving.

Remember John Dumay at Macquarie University, who I talked about at the beginning of this chapter? I did ask him what message he wanted to leave with all of you. Here is how he answered. "My role as an educator is to teach critical thinking and morality. One of the first times I taught sustainability, a brilliant female MBA student asked, 'Why are you telling me this? What can I do about it?' I told her, 'It's not about what you can do right now, but in five or 10 years, when you've finished your studies and you're in a boardroom, making decisions, you'll remember this lecture. You'll then have the power to make a difference using your knowledge and moral compass.'"[119]

LESS TALK, MORE DEEDS

I am going to stand on the shoulders of giants for the parting thoughts in this chapter. My own paradigm changed recently. Had you asked me 18 months ago what the opposite of "fragile" was, I would have immediately answered "resilient." I have a very different view after reading *Antifragile: Things That Gain from Disorder* by Nassim Nicholas Taleb and *How to Be an Antiracist* by Ibram X. Kendi. Among the many inspiring and informative messages in each book was a reinforcing construct. It is not enough to be either "resilient" or "not racist." In fact, these are neutral states of being, akin to being a spectator on the sidelines. "Anti" requires action, and in an oddly recursive way, it then becomes "pro" something else.

As Taleb so eloquently writes: "Antifragility is beyond resilience or robustness. The resilient resists shocks and stays the same; the antifragile gets better. My idea of the modern Stoic sage is someone who transforms fear into prudence, pain into information, mistakes into initiation, and desire into undertaking ... Let me be more aggressive: we are largely better at doing than we are at thinking, thanks to antifragility. I'd rather be dumb and antifragile than extremely smart and fragile, any time."[120]

And as Kendi so clearly articulates: "The opposite of 'racist' isn't 'not racist.' It is 'antiracist.' What's the difference? One endorses either the idea of a racial hierarchy as a racist, or racial equality as an antiracist. One either believes problems are rooted in groups of people, as a racist, or locates the roots of problems in power and policies, as an antiracist. One either allows racial inequities to persevere, as a racist, or confronts racial inequities, as an antiracist. There is no in-between safe space of 'not racist.'"[121]

Quite simply, it does not matter whether you are anti the shareholder supremacy model or pro human capital, sustainability and corporate purpose. You are a champion of change. Now is the time for more deeds and less talk.

EXPERTS WEIGH IN

CHAPTER 9

David Bookbinder Talks Valuation

Dave Bookbinder is a career-long valuation professional with a keen interest in elevating the practice of corporate valuation to account for human capital. Dave is a corporate finance executive with a focus on business and intellectual property valuation. Known as a collaborative adviser, Dave has served thousands of client companies of all sizes and industries. He is the author of The NEW ROI: Return on Individuals, *a #1 best-selling book about the impact of human capital on the valuation of a business enterprise.*

Dave is also the host of "Behind the Numbers," the show that digs deeper to understand what matters most in business. Dave writes about finance, leadership and the value of people as a contributor at TLNT.com, CFO University, Thrive Global and the Enterprise Engagement Alliance. He is also a former contributor to the business section of the HuffPost.

The following is his point of view in his own words, shared with me about People Eeconomics and how it relates to valuation.

FOR THE LAST 30 YEARS, IT'S BEEN MY JOB TO TELL COMPANIES how much they and their most-important assets are worth. Business valuation is driven by the numbers — and the assets that get the most attention are things like intellectual property, brands, patents, contracts … you get the picture.

But I'm here to tell you the most-valuable asset any business has is an asset that doesn't even appear on a financial statement: its people! A product is nothing without the people behind it building it, selling it and maintaining it. Even a company's brand is worthless without its employees delivering on that brand's promise.

During the worldwide pandemic, this was more evident than ever. There was shampoo and scissors in hair salons, but no stylists to use them. There were tools and machines in manufacturing facilities, but no people to operate them. And ironically, it was the people in some of the most-thankless positions, like delivery drivers and supermarket employees, who were being relied on to keep us all fed.

Here's the problem: We live in a throwaway culture. If something is broken, it's easier to dump it and get something new. Now extrapolate that concept into corporate America — if someone doesn't fit the mold it's easier to fire them than to find a different solution.

More often than not, when an employee struggles, it's the result of poor leadership. Not a lack of leadership — improper leadership. Let's talk about leadership. Every CEO on the planet says, *"Our people are this company's most valuable asset."* But they don't always behave that way. Maybe that's because this most-valuable asset doesn't show up on a balance sheet with the other assets. Employees are essentially treated as expenses through salaries and benefits.

During my career, I worked for some great people who led with empathy and for whom I'd walk through fire. Being a single dad for more than a decade, I really appreciated those leaders who understood that I had to deal with things that my colleagues didn't. I never asked for any special treatment — just the flexibility to manage the various aspects of work-life integration.

I also worked for others who didn't get it at all. I remember the eye-rolls and snarky comments like *"It must be nice to leave the office at 3 o'clock."* Yeah, nice. I'm going to pick up a sick kid from school and we'll probably be up most of the night. I also need to help the other kid with dinner and homework, and I'm still going to finish my job duties as well. Sounds like a party.

Have you ever felt like you were nothing more than a number on a spreadsheet to your boss? You see, they didn't understand the foundation for every successful business; priority number one: create an environment for happy, supported employees. Respect and support those human assets and you'll earn a more-dedicated and -effectual worker. That hits the bottom line.

It was through their poor leadership I learned first-hand about employee engagement and how it affects productivity, discretionary effort and — ultimately — bottom-line profitability. As I said, I'd do anything for those leaders who appreciated and respected me. They got my best stuff and the extra effort that comes with someone who's bought in. Those snarky leaders didn't deserve the going above and beyond — they reaped what they sowed.

But not all poor leadership is driven by character flaws or bad intentions. Many of these bad leaders just had bad role models. Maybe this is why they didn't get it: In the U.S., the average age when people become managers of other people is 30. The average age when a U.S. worker gets their first management training is 42. Think about it. Managers spend a full decade not knowing what they're doing ... and worse yet, doing damage. They're left to figure it out for themselves based on their own experiences of working for ineffective leaders.

Roughly seven out of 10 employees are still checked out at work, according to Gallup. Disengaged. Doing the bare minimum to get by. Even more damaging than the disengaged workers are the ones who have become toxic. They're not just checked out; they're trying to take you down.

Imagine if your business was a lifeboat with 10 people on board. Three people at the front of the boat are actively rowing to safety. Four people in the middle of the boat aren't rowing at all. And three people in the back of the boat are trying to sink it.

PEOPLE ARE INTANGIBLE ASSETS

When folks in my profession talk about determining the value of people, it is typically in the context of a business combination called a purchase price allocation (PPA). The PPA is an accounting exercise that requires the assignment of the fair value of all tangible and intangible assets and liabilities acquired in a business acquisition.

Human capital is considered an intangible asset, and a common way of ascribing value to people is through the assembled workforce in its entirety. The existence of a highly trained workforce in place saves an acquirer from having to go out and recruit, hire and train a new group of employees to effectively operate the business.

In calculating the value of the workforce, valuation practitioners will often use a Cost-to-Recreate method. The math behind the methodology is such that if we can estimate all the costs incurred to recreate the workforce, that total cost will reasonably represent the *value* of the workforce. For example, if "Ed in Accounting" costs $75,000 (salary, benefits, recruitment, training, etc.), the methodology presumes that we can find, hire and train another person just like Ed for the same $75,000.

As I've stated many times, I want to be crystal-clear that this is not a criticism of how valuation practitioners go about valuing human capital or how the accounting profession recognizes that asset. Intellectually, we are simply valuing a particular asset in a particular way using the available and accepted tools and methods.

My observation is, however, when valuing the workforce, some implicit shortcomings in the Cost-to-Recreate method come to the surface. First is the assumption all employees are interchangeable — that is, one Ed is just as good as another Ed in the same way that one computer or other piece of equipment is the same as and just as good as another. The second flaw is cost and value are one and the same. People are not commodities. We are not fungible. Cost and value are different concepts. Lastly, the Cost-to-Recreate method focuses largely on only the *direct* costs associated with replacing people, but never accounts for the impact they make on the company's bottom line.

Using Ed as an example, Ed's value to the company far exceeds what appears on his résumé, so the cost of replacing him isn't simply a matter of finding someone else with similar education and experience. Besides his thorough accounting knowledge, Ed also fully understands the organization's clients and has a thorough knowledge of its history. He can leverage this knowledge to boost the company's bottom line. Ed brings benefits to his employer that are likely to take his replacement weeks, months or possibly years to replicate.

THE REST OF THE STORY

There is more to the story than simply the costs associated with replacing people. Certainly, more than just the direct costs. According to data released by the Center for American Progress, the direct cost associated with turnover for an average employee is roughly 20 percent of the annual salary. For more-specialized personnel and executive-level employees, the costs can exceed 200 percent.

There are also indirect costs associated with replacing employees that aren't fully captured in the statistics. Such things include:

- The lack of productivity the employee exhibits once they've made the decision to disengage.

- The impact on remaining employees' morale as they question the reasons behind the departures/termination; and

- The real cost of lost productivity.

The real cost of lost productivity refers to the fact that while estimates can be made regarding when a new employee comes up the learning curve to reach a satisfactory level of performance, it doesn't account for the replacement of the nuanced things longer-term employees have learned over time — things like corporate culture and protocols, the best resources in the company for specific information, even the boss's preferences. Call it institutional knowledge, and it truly affects productivity. More importantly, the employees with institutional knowledge are valuable assets.

SHRM estimates the inclusion of indirect costs to employee turnover to be between 100 and 300 percent of the annual salary. There are also the opportunity costs of replacing an employee. A bad hiring decision can cost up to *five times* that employee's salary, according to SHRM.

Then there's the matter of employee engagement.

If we can agree engaged employees are more valuable than disengaged employees, then I suggest adding an "engagement coefficient" to this equation. A variety of tools can be used to identify who are the engaged vs. disengaged employees, so let's bake that into the math as a force multiplier (or reduction) to the employee value.

THE MOST VALUABLE ASSET

As I mentioned, this "most-valuable" asset doesn't appear on a financial statement; rather, it is subsumed into goodwill. Why do we value the assembled workforce? Because that recognizes that human capital interacts with other assets.

The intangible assets that land on a balance sheet, like trademarks and patents, are referred to as identifiable intangibles. They meet certain criteria regarding being legal or separable. Goodwill is the residual intangible value that's left after ascribing value to the identifiable intangible assets.

The assembled workforce is a contributory asset. Contributory assets are those tangible or intangible assets used in the generation of the cash flows associated with the subject intangible asset that is being valued. For example, in valuing a customer relationship asset, we deduct an "economic rent" for the use of contributory assets like fixed assets and the assembled workforce.

THE BIGGER PICTURE

While I happen to think there are ways to improve the valuation of the assembled workforce, until this asset is given its due on the balance sheet, there is ambivalence about making such improvements. The bigger issue here is the impact of human capital on the overall value of the business enterprise.

A multitude of studies documents companies that create a great place to work and have a higher level of employee engagement than their peers, and this translates into more productivity and higher stock prices. This means we know empirically that corporate culture, employee engagement and business value are all connected. As individual investors, we can buy shares of these great companies or buy mutual funds that have a strategy of investing in these companies. But for private equity firms or companies looking to make strategic acquisitions, there are other considerations.

One such consideration is the SEC's recent addition of human capital disclosures to the requirements of public registrants. While many believe the SEC went a little light and had hoped it would have settled on more-rigorous disclosures, it is worth noting that these new requirements were announced in the middle of a global pandemic.

These disclosures will be helpful to investors in thinking about where to allocate their capital. It's been said that greater transparency would allow investors to direct capital more efficiently to its highest value use, thus lowering the cost of capital for well-managed companies. Put a pin in that for a moment and we'll come back to why it matters.

VALUATION 101

The premise of business valuation is it's *forward-looking*, where value of a business (today) is equal to the present value of its expected future benefits, like cash flow. These estimated future benefits are converted into a current value through a mathematical technique known as discounting. The discount rate applied to the future benefit stream typically is the company's cost of capital, as defined previously. Considering the relative proportion of debt-to-equity in a company's capital structure is called the weighted average cost of capital (WACC).

WACC is defined by Investopedia as *a calculation of a firm's cost of capital in which each category of capital is proportionately weighted. All sources of capital, including common stock, preferred stock, bonds and any other long-term debt, are included in a WACC calculation.*

> *WACC = (Ke * %e) + (Kd * %d)*
>
> *Where:*
>
> *Ke = cost of equity, Kd = after tax cost of debt,*
>
> *%e and %d = proportion of equity/debt based on market value*

In that formula, the cost of equity component (Ke), using the Capital Asset Pricing Model, is:

> *Ke = Rf + (ß x RPm) + RPs + CRP + CSRP*
>
> *Where:*
>
> *Rf = risk-free rate, ß = beta, RPm = market risk premium, RPs = size premium, CRP = country risk premium, CSRP= company-specific risk premium*

That's it for the equations. Here's what's important: Investors want to be compensated for risk — the more risk associated with the investment, the higher the expected or required rate of return (also called the "cost of capital" or "discount rate"). The higher the discount rate applied to the future benefit stream, the lower the value of those future benefits. That is just how the math works. Each of the individual components in the cost of equity calculation is market-based and supported by empirical data except for one: the company-specific risk premium (CSRP).

There is debate in the valuation community about whether adding this company-specific risk premium is double-counting factors considered in the other components, but it is still widely accepted that there are risks inherent to a specific business that are not captured elsewhere in the cost of equity inputs. Thus, this adjustment is warranted.

Some of the factors valuation professionals consider when developing the CSRP include:

- Revenue and profitability growth trends

- Company financial risk

- Operational risks

- Customer, product and market concentration

- Relative competitive position

- Quality and depth of management team

Unlike the other variables, there are no market-based or empirical studies to refer to when estimating the adjustment factors for these elements, so the assessment of these, and other factors, results in a ***subjective adjustment*** to the discount rate based on the professional's experience and judgment.

When thinking about the SEC human capital disclosure requirements, I believe we will ultimately be able to directly correlate the impact of the investment in people to the company's stock price performance.

Again, greater transparency would allow investors to direct capital more efficiently to its highest value use, thus lowering the cost of capital for well-managed companies.

All other things being equal, a lower cost of capital (discount rate) will increase the valuation. A higher discount rate lowers the valuation. The greater the impact of the CSRP, the bigger the impact on cost of capital and on the valuation.

I believe the human capital investment, or lack thereof, must be considered in the determination of the CSRP, effectively adding another bullet point to the list above.

Many valuation professionals only consider the depth and quality of the subject company's management team when thinking about the human capital component in developing a CSRP; however, *all* human capital assets should be considered.

This could prove to be risk-mitigatory, thus lowering the company's cost of capital and *increasing* its valuation. I advocate for the inclusion of the human capital investment factor (HCIF) component in the calculus. Laura Queen calls it "people alpha" but we're talking about the same concept.

The equation, when modified to consider the HCIF, might look something like this:

$$Ke = Rf + (ß \times RPm) + RPs + CRP + CSRP \ (\text{-}/\text{+}\mathbf{HCIF})$$

HCIF becomes part of CSRP or perhaps even supplants the CSRP as a component in the cost of capital calculation.

There is growing momentum in people-centric investing, with new SEC reporting requirements regarding human capital disclosures along with a corresponding popularity of ESG investing and more. Doing well by doing good is not just an aspirational expression: It is a reality. I envision a day when human capital will be a line item on the balance sheet, and investors will use this modified cost-of-capital formula to calculate more-robust business valuations and to be better t separating the diamonds from the junk when buying these companies.

CHAPTER 10

David Griffith Talks Leadership, Boards, Poverty and Much More

Dave Griffith is a friend, neighbor, business advisor and thought partner. Conversations with him always shift my perspective. Sometimes he helps me galvanize my thinking; other times, he turns my world around. Every time, he inspires me. I reached out to him to tap his well of deep experience as an executive, an expert in organizational governance, a caring and committed public steward, and an eminently pragmatic business person. I shared the following writing prompt with him and asked for a chapter-length contribution to this book.

In her book The Six New Rules of Business, *Judy Samuelson shares the following quote from her friend, professor Lynn Stout. 'United States corporate law does not, and never has, required directors of public corporations to maximize shareholder wealth. To the contrary, as long as boards do not use their powers to enrich themselves, the law gives them a wide range of discretion to run the public corporations with other goals in mind, including growing the firm, creating quality products, protecting employees, and serving the public interest. Chasing shareholder value is a managerial choice — not a legal requirement.'*

Samuelson, who is from the Aspen Institute, later discusses PepsiCo's former CEO Indra Nooyi's leadership/governance philosophy, saying, 'Indra consistently reminds audiences to focus on how you make your money, not how you give it away. There is a role for philanthropy and good works, but to secure reputation among consumers and build trust with investors and regulators entails careful management of everyone who touches the product from development to delivery. And that level of vigilance requires a fundamental transformation of business mindset and processes.'

Some questions to consider:

- *In a world beset with pandemics, social and racial injustice, equity, equality, and pay parity issues, what are the roles of boards and board members for both public and private organizations with respect to business focus on human capital (e.g., should compensation committees become 'human capital' committees)?*

- *What needs to remain (current strengths) and what has to change in board oversight and governance, especially given the cry for greater transparency?*

- *In what ways do the roles of executives need to change? How can boards facilitate these changes?*

- *Is there a role for higher education in making necessary changes in board oversight and governance, management/leadership, skills and worldview as we make steps toward more-inclusive capitalism? If so, how can they serve this mission?*

- *How do purpose (or as Simon Sinek calls it, 'just cause') mission, vision and values factor into the equation?*

- *What about the makeup of boards — is there, or should there be, a role for employee representation on boards?*

- *What are your thoughts about the recent Nasdaq announcement requiring greater board diversity? Pros, cons, things to consider?*

- *What am I not asking that you think is important for the audience to consider?*

Dave and I traded a few emails to clarify my asks and then he suggested I take a tour of the blog posts he's been writing since 2014. These chronicle his journey from corporate executive to service at the helm of a nonprofit, faith-based organization in Philadelphia. As you will see, his words say so much more than mine ever could. What follows is a compilation of some of his writings — both blogs and emails (lightly edited for style consistency) — that either directly or indirectly address the questions above. Seeing the world through Dave's lens has been an incredible gift for me and one I hope will resonate with you, too. You can find more of his perspectives at www.wearmuddyboots .com.

HAPPY BIRTHDAY DAD (POSTED FEBRUARY 23, 2014)

My dad would have been 99 this February 28 had he lived. He passed away nine years ago, a few days short of his 90th birthday. This blog is named from a phone call between Dad and me when I was starting my first management job. I was a young manager for IBM in Pittsburgh. I called Dad to share my first day with him. He asked me to stand up and look down. What shoes are you wearing, he asked? My black wingtips, I answered. Wrong answer, you need to be wearing muddy boots.

His message was you don't manage from behind a desk. You go out into the field. Talk to customers, vendors, suppliers, employees closer to the customer than you. You learn by listening, asking what can we do better and what is your pain? You learn much by being curious, asking the why and the how. His wisdom was in knowing that people love to tell their stories; you just need to be smart enough to listen to them. Even wiser to act on them.

The boots are in the mudroom. Every day when I go to work, wherever I go to work, I put them on.

POVERTY, RACE AND PRIVILEGE (POSTED MAY 16, 2018)

Good morning. My name is Dave Griffith, I graduated in 1972 and served as a trustee from 2004 to 2012. Our two children are among the 12 Griffiths who have graduated from here since 1953. I went on to Kenyon College in Ohio, and then for 38 years worked in the for-profit world, the last 23 years with Modern Group Ltd. in Bristol, PA, an industrial holding company, where I remain chair. I also serve on several public and private boards.

I am currently the executive director and head coach of Episcopal Community Services. We are a 150-year-old social service agency focused on asking individuals, both participants and stakeholders, to Look Up and Challenge Poverty. We envision a world where opportunity is available to all. We do so on the bedrock values of Dignity, Community, Justice and Impact.

As an agency, we work with some 3,000 individuals a year. We are by design a learning organization and by design a thought leader in our space, and we advocate for change to public policy on a local, state and federal level. I am the first non-priest, non-social worker to lead the agency. I am called to this work in part because of some of the early lessons I learned here. Not all of them pretty.

For the record, I am also an old, white, business guy.

Up until five years ago when I started at ECS, I would never have identified myself that way. Having been directly involved in the agency's work has been an education and a wakeup call; these learnings have altered my perspective on poverty, gender and race in America and my purpose today is to share that perspective with you as students and you as faculty.

For many of you, this may not be a comfortable conversation. But it is a conversation that has to be had, especially, in the halls of education and in places like Westminster.

Let me ask you a few questions. If you would please answer me by raising your hand.

- How many of you own more than two pairs of pants?

- How many of you know where you will sleep tonight?

- How many of you know where you will sleep in a week?

- How many of you know where you will have dinner tonight?

- How many of you know if you were sick, where you would go for treatment and how it would be paid for?

- How many of you expect to go to college?

- How many of you have a home?

- How many of you have a home that is safe?

- How many of you expect a job at a living wage when you graduate with your degree?

For 15% of Americans, both urban and rural; white, Hispanic and Black, the answer to many of these questions is no.

This is in America, the wealthiest country in human history, with an average annual household income of $59,000.

It is important that to understand poverty, you understand some of the numbers, so bear with me for a moment and stay with me while I share with you some of the data. There are lots of myths about poverty; let's look at the hard facts. If you are like me, the data were part of my wake-up call.

Poverty in America is defined for a family of four at $22,900. A number not adjusted for inflation since 1972. Safety net support is available up to $34,000 regarding food with SNAP (Supplemental Nutrition Assistance Program); medical with Medicaid and CHIP (Children Health Insurance Program); childcare assistance, early childhood education, out-of-school time. However, the safety net programs in America decline $1.50 for every additional $1.00 earned.

In Philadelphia where I work, the poverty level is 28% of the population or some 400,000 individuals. Half live at 50% of the poverty level, and 100,000 are children under 18. In America, some 1.5 million people live on $2.00/day or less, many on safety net programs, but not all. Poverty and near-poverty cut across race, gender and age demographics.

Poverty in America in 1960 was 15%. Today, unadjusted for inflation, it remains 15%. Apparently, the War on Poverty has failed. One could, and I do, argue that the vast majority of social service programs in America are in the maintenance business. What they and all of us need to be in is the changing business.

In the Philadelphia region, the 14 federal and state safety net programs cost some $5.8 billion a year. Nationally, some 35% of the federal budget is allocated to this space. Despite all this funding and history, poverty is getting worse.

What is the "So what" of all these numbers?

Poverty will consume us as a nation if we do not deal with it as a nation — 15% (and I can argue for larger numbers) is a staggering cost to us as a nation. Left unchecked, the social, moral and economic costs are unacceptable and potentially a threat as critical as any we face. The economic gap is widening, and at some point, we will see social and economic unrest that will make 1968 look like a walk in the park. This is an issue that is very much part of your and my children's future.

What do we as a society do? What do you as a Westminster community do? You are already engaged in the surrounding communities; serving a monthly lunch in Hartford, running two summer academic programs here for underprivileged area students, sending students over spring break for community service projects, and — of course — your civic engagement courses. But I want to challenge you to raise the bar.

First, become knowledgeable. The roots of today's challenges are historical and influenced by deep-seated issues of economic justice, race and gender. While we hold the founders' words that "all men are created equal" as America's guiding light, our history, and frankly our actions, tells us a very different story both then and in today's context.

Poverty is not a choice. No one wants to live in poverty. In fact, some of the most- resilient people I know are participants in our program. Learn the root causes of poverty. Understand the differences between where and how you live, and someone in poverty. To go deep, understand the issues of housing and family stability, of wellness, of education, of financial literacy and workforce development.

The way out of poverty is a job. Not a minimum wage job at $9/hour without benefits, but a living wage of $26/hour with benefits. But a job at $26/ hour or better also starts with a core belief that opportunity, with all the perquisites, is available to all. Not handouts, but access. The blunt reality is that core belief is not true.

As an old white guy, let me name the elephant in the room. It's called privilege. Of course, the way out of poverty is a job, just like the one I got with IBM when I graduated from Kenyon in 1976. I worked incredibly hard to get where I am today. I didn't need welfare; I thought poor people needed to get off their rear ends and get a job.

The truth is I was born on third base, and I thought I had hit a triple. I had parents, a home, their network, education, access to opportunity. Yes, I executed when I got there, but a clear path had been laid out for me. Access to opportunity was and is available to me, for many in America, and not just those in poverty; this is directly and uncomfortably not true. For many, the truth is they can't even get into the ballpark. To be clear, I am proud of my accomplishments, but I can't and you cannot make the assumption that the "American Dream" is available to all in our country. Our future as a society depends on changing that reality.

Let's contrast my experience to that of one of our participants at ECS. Shelby (not her real name) is an African American woman living with her grandmother. She does not know her father and her mother is working the streets and on drugs. She is the fourth generation of her family to live in poverty. She attended a public high school where the attendance is 45%, and the graduation percentage is even lower. Fewer than 20% of her class will go on to get additional education. Her ambition was to work as a beautician because that was her experience. At 18, she is not sure where she will live when her grandmother is no longer around, and she contributes all of her income of $7/hour, 35 hours per week from two jobs and no benefits to help pay the utility bills and rent. She has been raped twice. Unlike many of her peers, she is not a parent.

Shelby is in crisis 100% of the time. No one in crisis 100% of the time can productively problem-solve, let alone lift themselves out of poverty. Placed in the same circumstances, how would you do?

I can tell you the same story 1000 times. Many more complicated, many more tragic.

Shelby does not want to be where she is. She sought us out at ECS and we are working with her; we are setting goals to move her out of crisis and put her on a path that will provide her access to opportunity and in time, real employment and the chance to break her family's cycle of poverty. Shelby now has ambitions to work in marketing and digital media, and is in a program at Philadelphia Community College to gain the skills she will need to reach this goal. Her paid internship is more than twice her last two jobs. All we did was provide a safe space, access to resources, and coaching for her as an individual with potential and the dignity that anyone deserves.

Get educated on the real story of poverty. Get the facts, not the political rhetoric that is so destructive on both sides of the aisle these days. Look at this issue not from your perspective, which frankly may be privileged, but walk with a heart that is open to justice, dignity, community and an overwhelming sense of fairness.

The second thing you can do is, when you can and have the opportunity, get involved. While financial support helps fund this work, the key to helping break the cycle of poverty is building relationships, mentoring and direct involvement. Every child is one involved adult away from success. For many in poverty, there is no such an adult, let alone an involved peer.

There are organizations you can join and work you can do. But please do not be a poverty tourist. If you do this work, meet people where they are; get to know them and their stories. Work when you are ready with professionals at an agency and learn to be a coach or a peer to an individual living in poverty. Remember that your experience is not their experience. Understand what it means to be privileged and do not judge. While the scale of this issue is daunting, it starts one individual at a time. Someone helped you. Pay it forward when the opportunity presents itself.

The vast majority of agencies and individuals in this work are in the maintenance business; they tell people what they need rather than listen. I have found if you ask, people will tell you what they need. Be a coach and help them set goals and achieve them. The best brain science tells us that individuals learning to set goals and achieve them move from crisis to control. In fact, the efficacy of such work goes from 30% to over 85%. As an informed volunteer mentor or peer, you can help do this. The lesson is in the story of the fishes: I can give a man a fish and he eats for a day. Teach him to fish and he eats forever. Join the movement, be an agent of change, teach people to fish, help people know what fishing is.

Finally, you can advocate in the appropriate ways available to you. Public policy and funding in this space are designed on science that is 20 to 30 years old and is built around the concept of maintaining people, not helping them change and lift themselves out of poverty.

You can advocate for fair housing, better education, no more regressive benefit funding as income grows. But the single best thing you can promote is employment, jobs and a living wage with benefits in America. The way out of poverty is a job. Poverty robs individuals of choice; choices economic well-being can provide.

With housing, education and workforce development, we can prepare individuals in poverty for the workforce, but where are the jobs? Yes, unemployment is at record lows, but a job at 40 hours a week at $26/hour with benefits and a 25-hour a week job with no benefits at $9/hour both count in the data as employed individuals. The working poor is a large number of the 15%. Understand and challenge the data, see the reality.

Advocate for job creation and job training, and critically, for individuals in poverty to have the training and access to jobs that are created. Right now, there is a lack of individuals in the trades at critical levels. Infrastructure is failing; fund it. New technology jobs, startups. We need incentives to be created that drive real employment and not just for some Americans, but all Americans.

Another elephant is the issue of race, gender and economic privilege. Economic privilege and access are not readily shared. We live in an investor, bottom-line, economy; we need to live in one where social impact is a significant element in an investor's criteria and not financial returns alone. I firmly believe government funding will not, on its own. change the level of poverty in America. Our history suggests that public/private partnerships drive the most-effective programs. Partnerships that leverage inclusion and drive social impact create successful solutions driven by the market. Not spending 35% of the GDP on safety nets could fund a lot of our other needs.

Your generation is the one that I hope will get this right. There is great power in inclusion and social impact investing, and you know it intuitively. Hold your elected officials accountable, vote when you are old enough, be an informed citizen — not just of America, but of the world

— and start now. When you are in a position to do so, hold your community, your employers and yourself accountable.

As an old white guy, it took me 60 years to learn what real equality really looks like. Diversity is a checked box on an EEOC form, inclusion is a seat at the table, social impact is a return that also drives social justice. Our best moments as a country occur when everyone has a seat and return is measured in part by social impact. One can do good and make a profit.

You can make that decision now. How you behave, what you say and write about matters. Every day and in every place. You and Shelby could have been each other, but for the luck of circumstances. Decide what you stand for, what is acceptable, and what your hopes are for the future, not just for yourselves, but the Shelbys of this country.

Understand your individual behavior on the issues of race, poverty, gender and privilege speaks louder long-term than any letter to the editor and it is something you control; no one else. Look in the mirror.

And finally, understand what happens here on the Hill is an extraordinary opportunity many individuals do not have access to, let alone are aware that such institutions exist. You can coast, or you can take what you learn here and challenge the status quo. Invest now, to be able to give back later.

I have come to learn that by doing and facing the uncomfortable, one learns the most, grows the most, and it is rarely fatal. Scar tissue from such experience is the best teacher. You can live in fear of people different from you or you can meet people where they live and find common ground. In doing so, you too can look up and challenge poverty. It is my working definition and implementation of Grit and Grace.

It is your choice. Choose wisely, but choose, knowing not everyone has the gift and privilege of choice. Respect that gift.

Thank you. It has been my honor to speak with you this morning.

EMAIL TO LAURA QUEEN (JANUARY 21, 2021)

Last week, I had the opportunity to speak to an assembled group of leaders of family businesses sponsored by the Delaware Valley Family Business Center. They asked me to share my perspective, AKA scar tissue, on the attributes of leadership observed over my years in business and my service as a board chair with privately held for-profit organizations.

I shared five core attributes.

Muddy Boots. Leaders who put on their Muddy Boots and go into the field and listen to the answers to two questions: How are we doing? What can we do better? Leaders do not manage the business from behind a desk. They listen to customers, competitors, employees, thought leaders, educators; to the people closest to the work. They seek outside advice and perspective.

Time. They are intentional with their time. "They do the important, not the urgent." They carve out think-time. They are curious. They find the pain and fix it. They invest in learning and talking with contrarians. They think not in the present, but three to five years out.

Elephants. They create environments where it is safe to name the elephants. They focus on the hiring and the care and feeding of talent. They work to be the dumbest person in subject matter areas. They understand a bunch of talented people are more valuable than one individual telling people what to do. The world needs inventors and implementers. They understand inclusion is a seat at the table and the bigger the table, the better the decisions. More than a seat is the value of a voice at the table. That is the true definition of diversity.

Personal Brand. People know what they stand for. They live their mission, their vision and their values. People understand what is their North Star. They are consistent. They are both firm and calm. They run *to* the fire, not away from it. People want to work for them. They care more about other people's success than their own. They put their crew first, and their crew knows it.

Balance. They understand while focus is important, so too is balance. They understand shareholders are not the only stakeholders, but so too are family and community, employees, vendors and customers. They understand and act as though they are part of a much-larger system and we all carry the responsibility to pay it forward. They do not put greed ahead of grandchildren.

In the end, leadership can be summed up in the concept of legacy. True leadership understands it is never about them. Rather, it is about the organization they lead and the people they serve. They understand the old African proverb, "To go fast, go alone, but to go far, go together." Leaders pull the rope; they don't push it. They understand that personal achievement and economic security is a function of stakeholder service. Value creation comes from the mix of all of these.

All of your stakeholders. Especially your future ones.

EMAIL TO LAURA QUEEN (JANUARY 2, 2021, FROM INC. INTER-VIEW ARTICLE[122])

After 37 years of working in the for-profit world, I was asked to lead a nonprofit social service agency in Philadelphia. Having made the switch from CEO to executive director, I get asked about the differences from individuals thinking about making a similar transition as a final professional chapter and what they ought to consider.

After six years, here is my list.

1. **Talent Matters.** In both sectors, the better the talent, the better the outcomes. Historically, nonprofits have had lower compensation and benefits, and the approaches I used to attract talent had to get retooled. While I have found investing in professional development, best-of-breed communication practices and an inclusive workplace — as in people who work for you have a seat at the table with strategy and problem-solving, all help attract and retain talent in both sectors. The great talent in the nonprofit

sector is called to this work. Discerning that call is critical in the hiring process.

2. **The Pace is Different.** Not for the challenges, amount of work and long days. Instead, the pace for getting answers from funders, government and in matters of compliance is very different. I am used to regulation, but in this sector, the amount of paperwork and the number of touches on any given issue is complex and at times lacks a sense of urgency. Persistent and, specifically, relentless patience is a necessary tool in the tool kit.

3. **The Myth vs. Reality of This Work.** I thought I was savvy about the issues of poverty, race, economic opportunity. After all, I had run a large business and was well-read and involved in nonprofits as a board member and volunteer. Never has the ability to listen, ask questions, talking to the people closest to the work mattered more. I would urge anyone to come into this work with an open mind and an open heart. Business skill can make a huge difference, but the program work is complex and layered. It took two years before I could start to connect the dots between poverty and race and privilege in this space and understand what mattered to move the needle.

4. **Collaboration is Not a Given.** Forty percent of the social service agencies in our region have six weeks of cash on hand. Most agencies depend on government funding for 90 percent of their funding. As an observation, most agencies do not naturally collaborate as a function of protecting funding. I think the ability to bring focus on the work, especially work that delivers impact, and to collaborate to produce a wide range of services is a skill where an individual with a business background can bring value. Joint ventures can bring terrific value to the individuals being served and drive impacts at much more effective levels.

5. **Data Matter.** I am used to using data to drive quality improvement. Getting data you can act upon is difficult in this sector and only now being recognized as critical to driving process improvement. Like the for-profit work, talking to your customers, finding the pain and addressing it is the key. In both sectors, we make the mistake of telling people what they need rather than asking.

6. **Overhead.** I ran a profitable business with 21% overhead as measured by GAAP and sit on several for-profit boards. Form 990s, if you believe them, suggest 8–10 percent in this sector. Funders are only now understanding that overhead is critical to successful programs. Finance, IT, HR, marketing, development all need to be done right so programs can function and focus on delivering quality impacts. Changes coming in GAAP will drive better accounting in the sector. Donors and funders will take some time to reset the model of what defines success. It is not the budget mix, but the impacts. The best agencies deliver impacts in the most cost-effective manner. Education about that mix is critical.

7. **Boards.** There is a significant difference between dealing with a paid board vs. a volunteer board. Board recruitment is critical in both sectors. However, with a volunteer board, there are different levers to consider when evaluating decisions, and with governance and nominations; while it should not be, it *is* different. Again, this is a space where a business background can add value. It is essential to look at skills, diversity of thought and experiences, funding capacity, and networking ability. The ability to have clear, transparent communications; hear from all views; have two-way feedback; and clear expectations is essential for an effective nonprofit board relationship with management.

8. **Focus.** It is easy to be pulled in many directions in both sectors. A critical skill is the ability to say no to your staff, your funders and board. Your heart will want to say yes. The key is the focus to drive impact, and it requires a clear vision and strategy. In nonprofit work, there is a tendency to chase funding. Mission, vision, values matter, and they should define your work and your direction. If they are right and they respond to real needs, then the funding will follow.

9. **Humble Experience.** It is easy to think the scoreboard you measured yourself on in business matters in the nonprofit sector. In many cases it does, but the program work is hard and is, by definition, humbling. I strongly suggest the better way to share experience is as scar tissue, in that when you made a mistake, you share what you learned, you continued to move forward. In most matters, a mistake is rarely fatal, and the sun will come up tomorrow. Experience is perspective and it is something you need to share from a frame of reference that matters to the people you work with.

10. **Muddy Boots.** If you know me, you know the story. You do your best work in the field with your muddy boots, listening to the people closest to the work and the people you serve. Ask how we are doing and what can we do better. And you listen. You listen with intention and without defense. I have long believed a leader is at their best in their muddy boots. This is true in any sector, for-profit or non-, and I could make the case is also true in life.

Finally, if you are not called to the work, I would strongly suggest you consider other options for a final chapter in your professional life. Understand what you are getting into and do it for the right reasons. But if you are called, there is no more-rewarding work. You work with amazing people and stakeholders; you have the opportunity to coach young people;

you get way more than you give; you learn and grow tremendously; and if you can move the needle in your space, make a difference, then the opportunity for a legacy that matters is significant.

LESS TALK, MORE DEEDS (POSTED ON MARCH 9, 2014)

I had a wakeup call this weekend. On Saturday, ECS, along with the diocese, hosted our first Partners in Outreach conference, an event months in the making. It exceeded all our expectations. More than 140 people representing 50 parishes from across the diocese were in attendance. From the opening worship service, with a powerful homily from the Bishop, to an inspiring keynote presentation and lively breakout sessions, everything went exceedingly well. The conference closed with my introduction of ECS Consulting Services, our forthcoming Diocesan Outreach Directory, our 24/7 Community Resources webpage of available support services and, finally, a new initiative — ECS Homecare, which upon its launch will provide a great option for seniors navigating the in-home care marketplace.

Sunday morning, I was still basking in the glow of success. I was scheduled to speak for an ECS Sunday at a church in Old City where I planned to share how inspired I was by the turnout at our event. On my way, I went into the nearby Wawa to get a cup of coffee. Coming out, I passed a man camped out in front of the store, holding a cup, asking for change. I walked right by, not looking for fear of making eye contact. Then I stopped dead in my tracks. The day before, I had made a well-received speech about less talk and more deeds in our common work of caring for those in need. Less than 24 hours later, here I was walking right past this man.

Kim Shiley, our chief advancement officer, calls these God moments. I turned around and walked back. I could see the front door of the South Street Diner from where I stood, so I asked the man to breakfast. He started to cry. We shared a meal, we talked, I listened. He clearly had emotional issues and as I am not a professional, I can't comment on his condition. What I do know is that he had a hot meal and a conversation on a Sunday morning. When we parted, we shook hands. It was not comfortable. This work is not comfortable, but that man outside the Wawa did me a tremendous service when he sat down to have breakfast with me.

Will you seek and serve Christ in all persons, loving your neighbor as yourself?

I will, with God's help.

As my dad wrote me so many years ago, "It is about putting yourself in the hands of a higher power and having the faith to let that power guide your actions. It is never about the talk; it is all about the deeds."

Less talk, more deeds. Every day.

As I reread Dave's blogs and emails, among other things, I am struck by the perennial nature of issues and concerns: homelessness, poverty, inclusion and diversity, education, the ease with which we objectify others. The need for measures and metrics, and public-private partnerships, to keep us moving forward. Our perpetual struggle over the same issues. Now is the time… less talk, more deeds, every day!

CHAPTER 11

J. Renay Loper Talks Diversity, Equity and Inclusion

J. Renay Loper is vice president of program innovation at PYXERA Global and on the boards of Girl Rising, Community Change and the Harpswell Foundation. PYXERA Global is a company that, for 30 years, has been creating powerful partnerships between the public, private and social sectors to develop innovative and sustainable solutions to complex challenges in 90+ countries. Renay is committed to social impact, responsible philanthropy and developing inclusive solutions with business materiality. She has a proven track record in building strategic alliances. Renay was a college intern for me. Every time she pops up in my social media feeds and I see the amazing person she is in full color, my heart burst with love and gratitude – she is a gift. I prompted her with the following questions:

- *What is your "just cause?" What is its importance and meaning for you?*

- *How do you define inclusion and diversity? What are the risks of homogeneity in businesses, communities, etc. (why should readers care about this)?*

- *How do issues of inclusion and diversity inform your choices as a consumer, retail investor, employee, employer, supplier, community member, etc.?*

- *Nasdaq recently announced requirements for greater diversity on boards of directors; failure to do so would result in delisting. What about this move makes you hopeful? What are your concerns?*

- *What, from your viewpoint, are the generational differences in perspective about inclusion and diversity?*

- *Would you share a story, from your personal experience, that you hope will inspire readers to a new view and action in inclusion and diversity?*

- *We've talked about the idea of being a "passionate pragmatist"; what messages do you want to leave readers with and what steps would you suggest they take to make meaningful strides in the areas you feel are most important — particularly in the business and investor communities?*

- *If there is a quote or saying you'd like to use as the header for the chapter, please share it. I'd love to include it as additional inspiration.*

RENAY'S QUOTE

"Diversity may be the hardest thing for a society to live with, and perhaps the most dangerous thing for a society to live without."

— WILLIAM SLOANE COFFIN, JR.

WE HAVE BEEN HERE ALL ALONG

These are my perspectives in a post-George Floyd world. It pains me to have to think about race and social justice pre- and post- a man, a Black man, who lost his life at the hands of police. May 25, 2020, was a tragic day that will forever be remembered as the day that Mr. Floyd died, sparking global protests about police brutality and racial injustices — specifically, injustices against Black people. However, before Mr. Floyd died, these issues were very much alive, but unfortunately, invisible to the untrained eye. Black and Brown people have been marching, protesting and fighting for justice on these very issues for *decades*. Sometimes with progress and most times without. But it seems that since the world quite literally stood by and watched Mr. Floyd lose his life, there is no denying race-related injustices exist, and therefore no turning back.

I am hopeful, optimistic even, that this time will be different. The energy is different, the atmosphere is different, the generations are different, the resources we have at our disposal are different, the expectations are different, the consequences are different. Things are different.

In the days and months immediately after Mr. Floyd's death, corporations crafted in-solidarity statements, made commitments, and wrote million-dollar checks to Black-this and Brown-that like never before — Historically Black Colleges and Universities, civil rights and social justice organizations, and more. All of it is wonderful — necessary even. But it is long overdue and not enough. The injustices are so deeply embedded in the fabric of our society that it will take quite awhile for the collective to understand the injustices, and then even longer to dismantle the systems that have housed them — and then … build new ones.

Most Black and Brown people I know around the world are exhaling — both with relief that the time has finally come where the world appears to see what has been painfully obvious to many for so long, and with sorrow and pain that it has taken this long and cost so much in the meantime.

ONLY ONE

In professional settings, including business and board meetings, I am often the only *one* in the room. The only woman. The only non-white, and therefore the only African American. And while I am in my 40s, I am usually the youngest. When in corporate meetings, I am usually the only one with non-profit and community-based experience; and in nonprofit meetings, I am usually the only one with business experience. If you are reading this, chances are you have been the "only one" of something along your career as well — and while I am not aiming to one-up anyone, I do invite you to reflect on the feelings you had when you were the only one. You may have noticed and dismissed it all in the same breath, or you may have noticed it and commenced an internal dialogue to assure yourself you belonged, and you had something of value to offer. For me, it has most often been the latter accompanied by self-censoring — careful of tone, intonation and volume not to offend anyone or come off as a woman driven by her emotions.

Throughout my experiences, I have been coached by teachers and mentors who all seem to have read from the same manual, with advice such as "You will likely be the only Black woman at the table, so you have to work twice as hard to be taken seriously" or, "Be careful not to be too opinionated so you won't come off as the *angry Black woman*" (it's a thing; Google it), or, "Don't wear your hair in braids; it's considered unprofessional and you will give people a reason to not listen to you," or "You sound White on the phone, so that will work in your favor," and "You're fortunate your name is easy to say, so HR won't know you're Black." The last two are personal favorites. It's almost like I am guilty until proven innocent — having to prove myself on all fronts before being accepted.

Being the only one is exhausting.

The argument for diversity, equity and inclusion (DEI) is a broken record, on repeat for decades — but one where the DJ has not paused long enough to look at the record to understand why it is catching on. According to Pamela Newkirk, author of *Diversity Inc.*, the business of diversity is a billion — with a "B" — -dollar industry. An industry revolving around trainings and assessments, and little on practical interventions linked to tangible outcomes. If you ask business leaders, many will say they are *honoring DEI* by increasing the number of diverse new hires (usually White women or Black men), providing diversity training, and maybe even encouraging employees to take the day off to celebrate Juneteenth or another culturally important holiday. The symbolism is nice, but by no means should be conflated with real progress.

When looking at typical steps taken by companies toward "diversifying," I always ask *So what?*

So what more women are hired; are they psychologically safe to share their perspective without having to think about the pitch of their voice? Can they be confident in knowing their contributions to the team are of equal merit to any of their male counterparts? Can they be certain they will be compensated and recognized (both with promotion and acknowledgment) the same as their male counterparts?

So what more Black, Hispanic, Asian, Native American professionals are hired; are they welcomed to wear their hair, or even clothing that reflects their heritage, without judgment or fear of different treatment? Can they be certain their experiences measure just as tall as those of their White colleagues who may have gone to Ivy League schools — or who may have networked their way into their roles? Can they be certain they will be invested in with access to leadership, mentors and sponsors in the same ways as other colleagues?

So what the company changes the color of its logo to be all-black (in solidarity with the Black Lives Matter movement) or even rainbow (in solidarity with the LGBTQ community)? How can women and minority-owned businesses apply for consideration to become preferred suppliers and vendors? Are there any mechanisms in place to support these businesses, encouraging them to thrive in the corporate ecosystem? Will they have access to the resources they need?

The above so-whats are merely examples; the list can go on. The real core of the question is about power. How does the power shift in the organization as diversity grows and improves? How are decisions made; whose voices contribute to those decisions? How are the voices counter to progress held accountable? Where does the power lie?

The point is diversity, equity and inclusion is a way of being — and for it to be a way of being, the power has to shift. It is not a buzz concept for strategy, business imperative to improve the bottom line or box to be checked. It is the lifeblood and ethos of an organization — it must be in the organization's DNA. If not, and the organization is not accountable to its words, employees and customers alike will see through the façade and act accordingly. Existing and potential employees will seek employment elsewhere, customers will exercise the power of "cancel culture" and stop patronizing the business — and probably attempt to unseat the company's reputation through social media blasts and more.

WE INTELLECTUALIZE DIVERSITY, RATHER THAN HUMANIZE IT

Any time people engage in dialogue about issues that matter and affect individual lives, it is a good thing. Especially when the intent of the dialogue is to understand history and the subsequent realities history has caused. However, when the dialogue stays at the rhetorical level or remains stuck in history, we fail to remember the humanity connected to these matters.

With the rapid ascension of race-related diversity and inclusion in the spotlight, I have seen more book clubs, webinars, workshops, essays and speeches trying to help the masses understand what the issues at hand are and how to speak about them, in a *sensitive* way. One that makes attendees, listeners and readers feel *comfortable*, or assured of their innocence in their participation and lack of complicity in unjust systems. Concepts and terms like allyship, white fragility, anti-racism, implicit bias, dismantling structural racism, emotional tax, BIPOC and microaggressions, among others, have become commonplace. And while these concepts and terms should be part of the realm of understanding in this space, they cannot simply live in the recesses of our minds or show up as talking points in meetings and crafted statements; rather, they must always be brought back to the underlying humanness.

For instance, take the simple concept of implicit bias. We know that implicit bias is something we all have. It is so deeply rooted in our psyche that we are not aware it is there and more importantly, how it manifests in our world view and behaviors. As we learn what implicit bias is, how do we go about accepting we indeed have it and then understanding how it shows up for us? Say in that 9:00 a.m. team meeting about sales and projections? Or in the conversation with a loved one where we are venting about our day and we recall the "idiot" who cut us off as we turned into the parking lot and who "probably shouldn't have been driving that nice car" anyway? Or when we are thinking about buying a new home in an up-and-coming neighborhood and we drive around it and get a "feeling" in our stomach when we see a lot of people who don't look like us — but we can't seem to put our finger on what the feeling is? Or when we find ourselves rationalizing certain decisions, comments or actions so they make more sense?

One of the most-challenging hurdles people need to overcome to humanize diversity, especially if it doesn't directly affect them, is to recognize and remove the automatic value judgment of good and bad. For instance, there is the connotation that implicit bias is a bad thing and a person who prides themselves on being self-aware may have a really difficult time accepting they, too, have implicit bias. We all do. In and of itself, it is not a bad thing, just a fact. It is what we do with and about our biases that drives true value.

When we intellectualize matters, we are being passive — taking the safe way to deal with the issues at hand; when we humanize matters, we are poised to take action — certainly for some, this feels like a greater risk. We must think of people first and only then consider the issues.

ABANDON THE MONOLITH

When we consider matters of diversity, our default setting is to think about racial matters quite literally in terms of Black or White. If we pause long enough to go beyond that binary, we *may* begin to consider other binaries such as men or women, homosexual or heterosexual, poor or not poor, and so on. For illustrative purposes, I am simplifying. The binaries certainly go deeper, depending on the constructs we are operating in (e.g., education, abilities and so on.)

I invite you to consider the complexities and dimensions of people as you think about diversity and abandon the concept of binaries and the notion of one or the other.

I believe the immediacy of generalizations and assumptions has fueled the long-burning flames of isms (racism, sexism, ageism, etc.). Like implicit bias, our minds seek to make sense of information very quickly and therefore categorize people, situations and events to instruct how we navigate daily life. One danger of this default mechanism is the lumping together of people — when categorized, opportunity, fairness. equity and even someone's chance of survival goes out the window.

I like to say that "people are not franchises." When you go to a franchise hotel anywhere in the world, your experience is supposed to be consistent. You know what the lobby will smell like, what colors the staff will wear, how they reference reward points and so on. Well, people are not like that. When you interact and learn about one Latinx person or community … you have interacted with *one* Latinx person or community — not all of them. It is important to keep in mind that no one group — race, culture, gender, etc. — is a monolith. There is never one-size-fits-all when considering diversity; there is diversity and *intersectionality in diversity.*

LEADERS LEAD FROM WHERE THEY ARE

Throughout my career, and more frequently as of late, I have seen leadership roles reserved for those with certain titles and job descriptions. In general, the organizations I have worked in typically reserve leadership (i.e., strategy development, problem-solving, decision-making, pace-setting, etc.) for those with a higher pay grade and with a title that does not scream "individual contributor." As companies scramble to define what diversity means for them and determine how they should be showing up in the world post-George Floyd, leadership on such issues has been reserved for those with titles such as Chief Diversity Officer, Chief People Officer, or anything with diversity or human resources in the title, for that matter.

When we perpetuate this way of thinking, we are likely to overlook leaders and influencers in our midst — the ones who are most affected by these issues, the ones who haven't felt seen or heard, the ones who have witnessed biased treatments, the ones who question why things are the way they are, the ones who — outside of the office walls — live a different life from the one you see in the office or on the Zoom screen. The ones who are most connected and passionate.

Based on my experience in the social impact space with conversations with peers and colleagues, some of the best ideas and solutions come from those who are experiencing the pain. They know exactly what is causing the problem, how the problem affects them, what the lack of a solution will do and how it *could be* addressed. They need to be heard, understood, empowered and supported — sometimes with resources; other times with access, or guidance, or space. I am not aiming to reduce deeply embedded injustices to a simple "Let X solve their own problems," where X represents any historically marginalized group; what I am suggesting is that those who are most affected must be part of the conversation toward developing and deploying solutions. Handouts, pity and charity are not needed; the destruction of current systems allowing the injustices to flourish is, combined with equal voice and consideration.

Let people lead from where they are ... sounds a lot like equity, doesn't it?

THE INTERSECTION OF BUSINESS AND SOCIETY

There are several schools of thought about the intersections of business and society. The role and purpose of business has evolved over recent decades, largely from shareholder primacy to multi-stakeholder primacy. The latter view continues to experience its own evolution — from corporate social responsibility to sustainable development to ESG accountability and so on. There are many books and studies on this topic, so I will not attempt to do it justice here. What I can offer is my perspective on this shift through first-hand experience.

I believe business influences society. Business creates society. Business feeds off and fuels society. How can we separate them? Businesses and their entire ecosystems — from employees to suppliers to customers to shareholders to lawmakers and so on — are inhabited by people. Individuals. Many of whom rely on business for employment, dignity, a means to meet their own basic needs. Yet, they have been forced apart for too long. Businesses have generally treaded very lightly when it came to social issues — even often remaining silent. This baffles me because it is as if businesses have mastered the art of being *of* the world but not *in* it. In a sense, being of the world means developed by people and making and selling things to people, but not in the world in the participatory sense — caring about those who developed the business, who make the things ... and who buy the things.

After Mr. Floyd's death, it became somewhat acceptable for the first time to speak openly about racial injustices and how the events made us feel. Many companies, forced by their employees, attempted to partici-pate in the world. I believe this tragic event was part of a perfect storm and came at a time when our senses were already heightened and our emotions were already raw (thanks to COVID-induced social isolation, remote work, proven disproportionate community suffering and so on). Whatever the case, we brought the pain, anger, confusion, all of it to work with us. It sat with us in Zoom meetings. It dominated the responses to "How are you?"

The experience was utterly undeniable for a majority of employees — not just the Black employees. When leaders witnessed the impacts of this incident on their people and society as a whole, they were forced to take notice (I encourage you to read on your own about how companies responded — see links in the resources section). There is no turning back; these events, along with several others since then, have blurred the lines even further. As long as people inhabit businesses, business and society will be bedfellows.

RESOURCES AND RECOMMENDED READING

- Lauren Weber. "Companies Have Promised $35 Billion Toward Racial Equity. Where Is the Money Going?" (December 21, 2020) *Wall Street Journal.* https://www.wsj.com/articles/ companies-have-promised-billions-toward-racial-equity-where-is-the-money-going-11608570864.

- Robin J. Ely and David A. Thomas. "Getting Serious About Diversity: Enough Already with the Business Case." (November– December 2020) *Harvard Business Review.* https://hbr. org/2020/11/ getting-serious-about-diversity-enough-already-with-the-business-case.

- Jonathan Capehart and Pamela Newkirk. Interview with Pamela Newkirk; release of *Diversity, Inc.* (November 24, 2019). Politics and Prose. https://youtu.be/WSljuz-mVxs.

- Chimamanda Ngozi Adichie. "The danger of a single story." (July 2009) *TEDGlobal.* https://www.ted.com/talks/

chimamanda_ngozi_adichie_the_danger_of_a_single_story?language=en.

- Adele Peters. "Inside Levi's stand against gun violence." (May 17, 2019) *Fast Company*. https://www.fastcompany.com/90346594/inside-levis-stand-against-gun-violence.

- "Police Departments Across Country Embrace Active Bystandership to Prevent Harm." (September 29, 2020). Georgetown Law. https://www.law.georgetown.edu/news/police-departments-across-country-embrace-active-bystandership-to-prevent-harm/.

- "Advancing Diversity and Inclusion." *Business Roundtable*. https://www.businessroundtable.org/policy-perspectives/diversity.

- Corporate Social Justice Scorecard: As you Sow https://www.asyousow.org/.

- Kimberly Papillon, Esq. "Module 3: Bias and Well-Meaning People." Georgetown University. https://nccc.georgetown.edu/bias/module-3/1.php.

CHAPTER 12

Karen A. Fenner Talks
Communicating Across Cultures

Karen Fenner is the founder, principal and Chief Culture Officer at Globally Speaking, a cross-cultural consultancy specializing in inter-cultural training for global companies and their managers. With more than 25 years of experience, Karen's focus is helping global companies work together more effectively when various cultural and language backgrounds are involved, especially after a merger or acquisition. Her ultimate goal is to Maximize Communication and Minimize Conflict™ by providing managers with essential cross-cultural tools instrumental to being effective global leaders. A frequent guest speaker and lecturer, she has been invited to speak at various Executive MBA programs as well as Fortune 500 global companies. She shared her thoughts about two questions: "Is speaking English all it takes to be an effective global manager?" and "What role does communicating across cultures play in leading effective global teams"?

"WHAT MAKES THEM TICK?"

The former CEO of Chrysler Corporation, Bob Eaton, asked this question when he realized he needed to engage a cross-cultural expert as part of the impending merger with Daimler Benz AG. He did not call the consultant to understand how Daimler Benz and Chrysler would best merge accounting and IT departments. Nor did he engage the expert to understand the German communication style, presentation style or problem-solving style. He called because he wanted to know how to best and most-quickly negotiate one of the largest trans-Atlantic mergers in recent history.

Unbeknownst to Eaton, the CEO of Daimler Benz, Juergen Schrempp, posed the identical question to the same consultancy: "What makes the Americans tick? How do they think and strategize?" Both men wanted a lifetime of cultural upbringing presented in about three easy bullet points "to clinch the deal." This is understandable. Those involved with such a deal feel the adrenaline; they recognize that products align, synergies abound and the market is ready for them.

These were two very smart, very experienced businessmen. However, just like countless other global managers, they were not willing to take the next step to make this international merger *permanently* successful.

The consultancy they addressed was experienced as well because their answer to both CEOs was: "Unless both of you meet in one room and accept that your management styles are going to be completely different from one another, we can't take you on as clients." "Meet in one room and talk about … *cultural* differences?" both men asked in surprise. "We are on the cusp of one of the largest trans-Atlantic mergers in history. This will change the global car industry forever."

As we all know, the merger between Daimler and Chrysler did not produce the outcome investors had hoped for. Not taking the time to integrate the two cultures from the start and neglecting two very different styles of doing business caused the majority of American managers to ultimately leave the company. A very expensive mistake; a "merger of equals" ended up being the ultimate case study for cross-cultural disasters.

No matter how digitalized and globalized we become, or how quickly we can set up a Zoom meeting with four different nationalities appearing on our screen, business will always remain a transaction between people. The time we take to truly understand the cultural background of our international counterparts, to build trust and empathy for each other's cultural behaviors, is what ultimately creates a successful outcome in the world of global business.

I often make this comparison. Imagine two people — Tom and Kate — are engaged to be married. They're made for each another. They both have careers in the same industry, love to travel, love the outdoors. But Tom really wants to have kids and Kate … it's just not part of her long-term plan … That's OK; they'll figure it out once they are married, right? No, no, no …

The most-important component to any successful relationship is trust. However, when working with very different cultures in the corporate arena, trust is established based on different criteria. With some cultures, trust can be based solely on the reliability of facts, numbers, data. With others, it can be investing in getting to know one another, breaking bread, dedicating time to establish the foundation of a long-term relationship. Ultimately, what we must understand is when companies merge, even if there is not an international component, employees quickly sense the rules have changed, but don't know *what* these new rules are, *who's* making them and *whose* rules they should actually follow. These questions must be addressed at the beginning.

Years ago, I submitted a question to Jack Welch (former CEO of GE) and his wife Suzy Welch's advice column, which ran in *Business Week* for a number of years. I was curious about his thoughts regarding the effect culture has on companies and why it is too often neglected. My question was, "Why don't companies address the need for cross-cultural training until it's too late?" Lo and behold, Jack Welch picked my question, and his answer was printed in the following edition.

"You can't crunch culture," was his reply. That's it? I thought. You can't crunch culture? But then I got it. When companies are in the heat of the deal and the excitement of a possible merger or acquisition is on the horizon, people want the merger to go ahead. The deal must go on! In any merger, you can *crunch* the *numbers*; you can quantify the synergies resulting from the integration of departments, combination of supply chains, reduction of suppliers and consolidation of products; you can estimate successful outcomes on paper — but the integration of the people, a key element to a successful merger, can't be quantified. When neglected, the costs of dysfunctional teams, missed deadlines, departing employees and failed products can run up huge costs, including the ultimate cost: failure of the merger. All of this applies to Daimler Chrysler.

Culture runs the gamut from making eye contact with someone to how we toast when at a bar after work hours with our colleagues. An MBA student once told me about how he moved from Morocco to Belgium as a young child. He was always a class clown and continued his antics after moving to Belgium, which prompted his teacher to give his mother a call. After making it very clear to the mom that her son's jokester behavior was not welcome in her class, she ended her tirade with, "And your son did not even have the decency to look me in the eye while I was reprimanding him." His mother calmly answered, "Actually, my son was showing you the utmost deference and respect." The teacher did not know that in many African cultures, a younger person or someone with a lower rank making eye contact with the higher-rank person is considered disrespectful and rude.

A manager from Niger I worked with once said something similar. "I had to learn to make eye contact at the age of 26 when I came to the States." Imagine the conscious change he had to go through, starting his life in the U.S., and how his lack of eye contact could have been misconstrued. For Western cultures, someone who can't look us in the eye creates a lack of trust and even a sense of suspicion. Making eye contact is also pivotal when toasting one another in the German culture. One must make eye contact to truly be "breaking bread" and showing recognition and respect for the other.

Every culture has its own rules that have to be applied and adhered to when building a successful relationship. Disregard those rules and the intended outcome is jeopardized.

I experienced first-hand the dysfunctionality a lack of cross-cultural training can create when I was engaged by one of the top-five global medical device companies to work with a global product marketing team after an acquisition. The team consisted of Germans and Americans working together in the U.S., and everyone had good intentions. All involved wanted a successful product launch, but their way of getting there was so completely different from one another that they eventually experienced a complete communication breakdown.

Here are some of the obstacles they faced, my interaction with them and how these problems could have been avoided.

1. TIMING

I was approached by the company directly after the acquisition took place, which is the perfect time to conduct a cross-cultural training seminar with all parties involved. This is how communication breakdown is avoided, since we now have the opportunity to shed some light on everyone's cultural behaviors, from communication to hierarchy to socializing style. After doing this for many years, I can tell you countless "Aha moments" are experienced during this training. However, since not all German managers were able to travel to the U.S. right away due to time constraints, the training was put on hold. The team waited *one year* after the acquisition to finally conduct an inter-cultural immersion seminar and by then, the lines had already been drawn. Two "camps" existed on this team and I was brought in to establish unity in the clashing of cultures.

2. KNOW YOUR OWN CULTURE FIRST

The first thing I tell my clients when embarking on a project with another culture is to *know* your *own* culture and your own cultural nuances *first*.

Only then are you open and ready to understand another culture, receive it, understand it and work with it effectively.

If you are an American about to work with a Swiss pharmaceutical company, don't dive into books written about Swiss (Swiss German) management style. Read about the American management style *first*. Ask yourself, "How do I communicate as an American?" Do I engage in small talk on a Monday morning until 10:15 a.m., when the meeting was actually scheduled to *begin* at 10:00 a.m.? Unbeknown to you, you may have already annoyed half the people in the room by not respecting *their* time and starting the meeting punctually at 10:00 a.m. The Swiss and Germans are a punctual culture. Americans are a timely culture as well, but small talk and niceties are the oil that keeps the dialog, and ultimately business, flowing in the U.S. Not engaging in this is almost considered rude and not conducive to a good working relationship.

Sharing your vacation information in too much detail within the agreed-upon time frame of a scheduled business meeting would also be considered inappropriate and lacking seriousness in a number of European cultures.

If you are an American, another question you may ask yourself is, "Do I incorporate humor into my meetings — a little joke?" Not a bad thing; I always welcome it. That was, however, another problem with this team. Germans misunderstood the Americans' humor as not being sincere and not understanding or respecting the severity of the dismal results the team was experiencing. The American team leader's approach was to start the meetings with some humor to ease tensions in the room, help everyone feel at ease (or so he thought) and create a sense of unity. Humor is part of the social fabric of the United States and often seen as a good tool to bring people together, but it was perceived by the German managers as not taking the issues seriously. I am often asked whether Germans have a sense of humor. Of course they do, but business and social interactions are separate, not intended to be mixed. If both sides had recognized their own distinct cultural nuances first, they might have adapted their approaches right at the start of the project creating a unified bicultural team.

3. THE IMPORTANCE OF LANGUAGE: "DON'T WORRY, EVERYBODY SPEAKS ENGLISH"

Since the Germans spoke English, the teams on both sides were lulled into a false comfort zone, believing everyone was on the same page. This happens frequently in global business, independent of the nationalities involved, but is never the case because every English speaker is still driven by their own cultural background. Americans must ask themselves whether a German really going to stop being *German* — being very direct, extremely data-driven, not engaging in small talk, *just* because they are speaking English. The answer is most definitely not.

Americans have to realize that they may need to speak slowly when talking to "non-native" speakers and refrain from using the many idioms, specifically sports terms, that are part of the daily American lingo. "It's time for us to step up to the plate, put our game face on, and knock the ball out of the park." What in the world does that mean to a non-native English speaker? Absolutely nothing. This is not always easy, and I have to review my own lectures and presentations before I address a global audience.

Europeans often feel a false sense of confidence when working with Americans and that can also backfire. The mindset of Germans and others can be, "Hey, I vacation in the States all the time. I've been to Disney World, rode down Route 1 in California and pretty much only listen to American pop hits on my iPhone. I also binge watch Netflix on the weekends, so I have a pretty good grip on American culture." Highly unlikely. You only truly get a grip on a culture when living there and receiving a paycheck in that country.

Language, in an intercultural setting, plays a pivotal, often neglected role in understanding and relationship-building. For example, the German language is much more literal. Americans throw "heavy" words around in a light way: "love," "hate," "kill." "I love you for getting me that cup of coffee." Wow, love happens fast here in the U.S., a European visitor may think. Native English speakers need to remember they are fortunate enough to speak a language that can be used in almost every corner of the globe, but we frequently forget how difficult it is for non-English speakers to perform at their highest level while speaking a foreign language.

I worked with a French manager once who said, "During a meeting in my NY office, I wanted to make a point, but by the time I came up with the correct verb conjugation, the conversation had already moved on." How frustrating! We need to *respect* the language barrier, recognize how difficult it is for non-native English speakers to maintain quick-wittedness and spontaneity — only with this mindset and this empathy can the communication lines remain open.

4. PROBLEM-SOLVING APPROACHES

The 80/20 problem-solving approach versus the 100% approach created an enormous problem for this team. What do I mean by 80/20 vs.100%?

When Americans meet to discuss a project, a budget, a marketing plan, they may iron out kinks and strategize but are anxious to *get going* — "Time is money" as coined by Benjamin Franklin. Paralysis through analysis is not the approach Americans like to take. They want to start implementing what was discussed in the meeting immediately; in other words, hit the ground running, even if this means only 80% of the issues have been tackled. Americans think, "We can always meet again in a week, check in with one another. Change is inevitable — markets change, data change, people change their minds."

Not a plan for a German. When Germans discuss a marketing plan, a budget proposal or product development, they work out *all* potential problems 100% at that initial meeting. An enormous amount of data is presented, and an ultimate plan is put in place. Their presentations are filled with bar graphs and charts that sometimes go back three to five years because they want to understand, "How did we get here?" I often tell my

American clients presenting in Germany, "Even if you do not incorporate it directly into your presentation, at least have material and budgets ready from previous years. Be ready to talk about these items in great detail." Ask any German executive about the *best* way to do business with a German company and they would tell you, "Be prepared." Know your facts and your numbers inside and out, and have them with you. You will gain a German's respect for your thorough preparation and you will have laid a foundation of trust. Germans don't "wing" it, and they will immediately sense if you are doing so.

Americans often want the initial nuts and bolts of a project or concept. Does that mean they are not detail-oriented? Absolutely not. However, the details may have to be discussed at a later date. Within this team, the fact that the Americans did not discuss everything in detail from the get-go was seen as glossing over items, perhaps being sloppy or inexact. If both sides agreed on a structure for their meetings, possibly a *brainstorming* session on a Monday morning, and a more-detailed, *structured* presentation at the end of the week, both sides would have felt their styles were recognized and considered.

A final element that came into play was respect for *processes*. In this case, the Americans were working with the "founding fathers" of process and the Germans definitely did not feel the need to start omitting steps now. If Americans considered a step unnecessary, they wanted to skip it. This did not work for the Germans on the team. Even if Step B was not needed to get to Step C, a well-run German team would not omit it, since it was created for a *reason*. Therefore, it had to remain a vital part of *the process*. This German rigidity drove the Americans on the team crazy and was seen as being uncooperative and wasting time.

Americans considered this side of the Germans to be inflexible and difficult to work with. In addition, since the German managers felt everything had been *agreed* to at the initial meeting, they could work independently, with no need for additional meetings or an exchange of additional ideas. "We don't need to be babysat," one German manager told me. I tell my German clients that if you want to do business in the United States, you have to learn to be flexible.

5. COMMUNICATION STYLES

"You are wrong," said the email an American manager shared with me. I honestly had to hide a smile because the German who sent this probably thought she was being the most helpful, cooperative and honest co-worker by providing such "constructive" criticism!

Yes, when working with a very monochromatic culture[123] such as the German culture, honesty is the best policy. Social and corporate relationships are two separate entities, therefore being brutally honest should not affect the working relationship. Germans feel they are not there to try to win a popularity contest or make friends — that comes after 5:00 p.m. They are there to be efficient and productive, and create a positive outcome. That sort of communication style works very well in Germany: efficiency, thoroughness, honesty, facts. Yet, this type of "direct" critique can be unsettling for Americans who come from an environment that values the adage, "If you don't have something nice to say, don't say anything at all."

Of course, Americans offer critiques, especially if a presentation did not hit the mark. A U.S. manager would preface it with something positive, though: "I appreciate the work you put into this ...," followed by, "However, I think we may need to look at this from another angle." By reinforcing positivity, the person on the receiving end is open to suggestions.

When I worked with this team, the Germans' directness was one of the major complaints Americans expressed. One U.S. manager openly said to a German in the room, "I resent the way you continually correct my mistakes in front of others." I must admit, the German manager was a somewhat difficult person, and not everything can be attributed to cultural differences. His unwillingness to soften his critical feedback made the already-tense climate worse.

This difference in communication styles was *fundamental* to the problems this team was experiencing. Germans were labeled as rude and impolite, whereas they saw their input as helpful and constructive. For Americans, being sharply critiqued in front of peers in a direct, blunt way made it difficult to build solid working relationships. Does this mean Americans need 100 compliments before the actual critique is voiced? No. However, I do tell my clients, especially German clients, if they want to be effective, maintain their audience and be part of a productive global team, they need to change their approach.

When traveling to Germany, I think it is imperative that Americans expect and are able to handle this blunt honesty. However, when doing business in the States with Americans, Germans need to learn to adapt as well. Changing the delivery of a message plays a role in ultimately having a change implemented. If the team had just been aware of these differences in communication style a year earlier, deadlines and two subsequent product launches would not have been missed.

CREATING A "THIRD CULTURE"

These are just a few items that became stumbling blocks to this team getting along and becoming a productive unit together. As you can see, so many of the issues this team faced could have been avoided with some initial cross-cultural training. The training would have revealed how different their approaches were and how to reach consensus about how to best create a *shared* culture based on *jointly* created rules and guidelines. I call this a "third culture" — one that covers items such as meeting style, frequency of meetings, being aware of each other's communication style and feedback. In the world of cross-cultural communications, a little goes a long way. Through maximizing communication, we minimize conflict.

REAL-LIFE IMPACT

CHAPTER 13

Turning Around a "Hot Potato" Plant

I'D LIKE TO INTRODUCE YOU TO MIKE, SVP OF OPERATIONS AT a company I will call Maxfield Pharmaceuticals. Historically, Maxfield production facilities have been considered the cream of the crop: highly productive, they routinely gain the highest marks during regulatory and quality inspections, are efficient and reasonably profitable. Unfortunately, this is not true for Maxfield's recent acquisition. Maxfield's new location has struggled with performance issues. At one point, the plant had been shut down by regulators for quality failures.

Mike and his team referred to the new plant as the "hot potato" because it had been tossed from division to division under its previous owner for more than a decade before Maxfield bought it. It was normal to see a rock propped in the employee entrance door so people without badges could get into the building, despite the fact they manufactured opioids. Mike had to fire the security manager because he and two of the contract security guards were selling marijuana out of the security guard post at the entrance gate. Three members of the HR department and the site controller were fired for illegal hiring practices and misappropriation of funds.

A well-regarded industry leader, Mike has a long history of turning around poorly performing facilities in pharmaceutical and chemical manufacturing. A retired Marine with significant frontline experience in the Middle East, he is an imposing figure who runs a tight ship. Although not much of a talker, when he speaks, everyone listens. His directions are clear and concise, well-thought-out, and leave no question about his expectations.

Every morning, seven days a week, he or his managers hold a team huddle. Each department sends a team lead or supervisor to report on their work unit and take notes on production changes, inventory shifts, general operations and other items of interest. They review every plant KPI — raw materials inventory, manufacturing output, quality metrics, sales forecasts, absenteeism and employee performance. Each department representative is responsible for sharing what is happening with their team and taking back to the team all the information shared during the huddle.

Operating details discussed during these daily briefings form the backbone of reports Mike shares with his executive peers and make up a substantial portion of the overall information provided to stakeholders as part of the company's communications initiative. Maxfield prides itself on inclusive capitalism, striving for transparency in reporting and capturing feedback from stakeholders in and outside the organization. This is one of the reasons Mike joined Maxfield.

Over time, Mike and Maxfield have discovered tremendous value in selecting measurements and metrics that make the difference in their operation and provide meaningful data to their stakeholders. Reporting consists of operating, quality, financial and human capital data. This information is provided to employees in interactive quarterly town hall meetings and via internal dashboards, accessible anytime in Maxfield's online communications portal. External stakeholders participate in quarterly update calls with the executive team and board-of-directors; they are also invited to participate in customer and supplier focus groups. Employees participate in surveys, as well as other informal and formal opportunities designed to hear their voices and enlist their support in promoting innovation.

Early reviews from the team at the hot potato are mixed. Some of the staff loves Maxfield's direct style and clear standards; others are downright hostile toward the ideas of accountability, disclosure and transparency. Even in these early days, the impacts are clear. The new plant is making huge strides: Quality, compliance and adherence to production schedule data show meaningful upward trends. Absenteeism is down by double-digit percentages and the plant has had no recordable safety issues in the past 90 days. Some employees remain skeptical, yet overall employee trust scores are up significantly. The facility has a long road ahead, but skillful selection of the right measures and consistent, transparent communication are reaping rewards for Mike, Maxfield and all their stakeholders. Together, Mike and Maxfield have proven the value and importance of metrics, measurement and transparency.

CHAPTER 14

Let the Buyer Beware

MERGERS AND ACQUISITIONS OFTEN INCLUDE WRITTEN AND unwritten terms and conditions. I once worked on a deal that included the explicit, unwritten condition that certain members of the acquired company would have significant roles in the newly combined organization. These individuals were personal friends of the former founder and CEO, and he felt compelled to ensure they were "taken care of" in the transaction. This is not an especially unusual ask, and part of my job was to evaluate and recommend roles for acquired employees when we were going through transactions.

There are any number of important considerations when making such decisions. Will adding this person create a redundancy? If so, how will this be handled? How do each incumbent's skills, capabilities, styles, alignment with culture and values correspond with the criteria for success in the role? What are they known for in their respective organizations — do they help people grow, are they technically expert, have they left a wake of painful employee encounters in their path? Where is the newly combined organization headed — is one candidate better suited to helping the business evolve?

In this case, we had embarked on a years-long initiative to carefully cultivate a positive organizational culture, craft a compelling vision, align talent and activities with our values, and measure employee engagement. Executive placements were a key aspect of these efforts and there was still important work to be done. We already had a leader in this role, a relatively long-service employee who had been a poor performer and was not a champion of the company's culture. On the surface, this appeared to be an opportunity to make a needed change.

In the very early stages of due diligence on the company we intended to acquire (the target), we had been given remarkable access to the employees, particularly other members of the executive and second-level management teams. This access allowed for meaningful conversations about employees' experience, leadership styles, culture, typical measures of performance and success, and other important aspects of the business. I learned the target organization was managed top-down, very autocratically and with little or no transparency below the second leadership level in the organization. Employees had little autonomy and decision-making was not delegated to lower levels. Discussions were made behind closed doors and debate was discouraged. The CEO and his small group of direct reports held most of the power and control, often wielding these like a weapon.

Our two organizations could not have been more different. We maintained organizational charts primarily for the purposes of compliance, data management and approving payroll. Employees were empowered and autonomous; they were expected to contribute ideas and suggestions, refine processes, and make decisions with little regard to their hierarchical level. When team members were invited to meetings, they were expected to voice opinions, debate openly and take action with virtually no follow-up. Things here happened fast, sometimes chaotically, and employees who enjoyed this style thrived.

Red flags about process, culture, leadership and measures of individual success popped up everywhere. When asked for my assessment and choice of options, I emphatically suggested we start with a clean slate and use the acquisition as an opportunity to redesign this part of the organization, provide access to one-on-one coaching and transition support for both leaders, and begin a search for the right person to fill this critical position.

Ultimately, the executive from the target company was offered the leadership role, despite my advice. He was selected for his advanced technical skills and reputation as a capable negotiator, with a history of highly effective cost containment. Mostly, he was chosen because of his relationship with his former boss, who would also be taking a position on our combined company's board.

Less than a year later, his department had experienced more than a 35% turnover, including previously high-potential staff members who left to take positions with competitors. We were embroiled in pending legal actions for allegations against him, including a potential class-action claim. One of our largest vendors had hiked prices sky-high to compensate their teams for having to work with him on our behalf — vendor-imposed hazard pay. Estimated costs for having to address the legal actions alone were well into the millions, including attorneys' fees and court costs.

The impact on employee morale, poor performance and resulting loss of talent for working in an unhealthy work environment was calculated at more than $4 million USD for this one year. We suffered a significant erosion in our reputation as an employer of choice, which made replacement hiring extremely difficult. Eventually this executive had to be terminated, and it took years for the company to recover from the damage created by this one poor decision. Some of the affected employees will tell you they still have not recovered from their experiences. Let the buyer beware!

CHAPTER 15

Voices Carry

"What would make this organization/team even stronger?" Questions are powerful. Used well and with positive intent, they can be the wrapping on gifts of incredible value. What follows is the story of one such gift shared by Kyle, a production facility general manager, about work my team assisted him with.

WE WERE TWO-THIRDS OF THE WAY THROUGH A DAILY integration team meeting and Jacob, the project management lead, nodded to Maria and Alessandra, our human capital consultants. They had asked for time on the agenda to review some of their team's findings. We were all eager to begin the process of planning for the day our deal with ABC would close. Each week started with the expectation that final signing was going to happen on Friday, but by the time Thursday afternoon rolled around, we knew there was at least one more week to go. It was a running joke and felt a bit like we were caught in the movie "Groundhog Day."

Alessandra thanked Jacob and the team for providing time on the agenda and then turned things over to Maria. "Thank you, everyone; it's great to spend time with you, again," she said. "Most of you have copies of our final report and Closing Day recommendations, but we thought it was important to share some details about how we came to our conclusions. During our focus groups with the team at ABC Pharma, we asked questions designed to help us understand strengths and capabilities, and identify opportunities for greater levels of performance and productivity. All from the employees' perspectives. 'What would make this organization/ team even stronger?' was one of the questions we asked."

Maria told us the employees were very engaged in the conversations and eager to share stories about their experiences. I had glanced over their report before this meeting. Some of the recommendations seemed like no-brainers, but a few seemed odd and even a little silly. I was curious and a little skeptical about the importance of their highest-priority Day 1 recommendation: Install Wi-Fi signal boosters.

It was no surprise to me the employees had identified Wi-Fi signal strength as an issue. I had to leave the building to receive messages or take calls from my cellphone. The building had been built in the 1960s of steel reinforced concrete and cinder block. It was frustrating for me, and I had only been dealing with it for a few months. I'd heard grumblings from the staff on a number of occasions, but employees needed something to complain about. I chalked it up to sour grapes and went on about my business.

I must have had "the look" on my face in this meeting. Maria paused, looked at me, and asked if I had any questions or concerns before she began. I began to shake my head "No," but stopped. "Yes — yes, I do. Your top priority for Day 1, Closing Day, is to install Wi-Fi signal boosters. It seems to me that there are a hundred more pressing things we should be doing on our first day."

Alessandra chimed in, "You're right, Kyle. We thought so, too. You are spot-on to call this out. Maria, would you mind starting here with your discussion?"

"Of course," Maria said. "I'd be glad to. Like most of you, the employees' concern with Wi-Fi signals wasn't a shock to us. We couldn't get a cell signal, send a text or check emails anywhere in the building! But we know that when these opportunities are brought up, there's more to the story, so we got curious and asked the teams to tell us more."

It turned out that team loved the roll-out of ABC's new corporate quality training, but the programs were delivered via streaming audio and video, and the bandwidth was so poor, no one could take the required training inside the building. The staff had choices. They could simply not take the training, which was a really big issue. The training content and records of having completed the training were required by the Food and Drug Administration (FDA). Failure to do so could result in sanctions that would cause harm to the business.

Various workarounds were happening. Some staff opted to drive 10 miles to the next-closest company location in their own cars on business time. At a minimum, this posed liability risks. If an employee had an accident during this time, it would be a work-related situation. Other team members drove to the closest public hotspot, a local restaurant, to use its unsecured network, again driving their own cars on business time to get there, not to mention potentially causing cybersecurity and data protection issues.

Maria said she and her team had done a quick back-of-the-envelope calculation. Most employees had to complete 10 trainings per year. If they chose to do the trainings by road trip, it cost the business five hours of lost productivity per training per employee per year. They estimated the impact in lost productivity alone at more than $320,000.

Average Employee Salary for this Location	$45,000
Average Hourly Rate	$21.63
Number of Trainings per Year	10
Number of Lost Hours per Training (travel, set-up, distractions, etc.)	5
Productivity Costs per Employee per Year	$1,081.50
Total Number of Site Employees	299
Annual Productivity Cost	$323,368.50

Maria said she had already spoken with Hal, our chief technology officer, who estimated the costs of fixing this issue at approximately $350, including installation labor. Installation would take about two hours and could be completed within hours of legally closing the deal.

"Okay," I said, "now I get the impact of this issue." I was annoyed I was facing a situation I hadn't understood or even cared enough to connect the dots on. "But why is this so high on the priority list? Don't get me wrong — this would be a huge boost to our ability to meet the immediate financial synergy targets for this deal, but we've got bigger fish to fry."

Maria responded immediately. "We want all of you to be truly successful after you've closed this deal. Success will largely depend on how quickly you can bring your new team along, and a key ingredient to this recipe is *trust*. Helping them buy into your processes and all of the changes that will happen over the coming days, weeks and months will require your new employees have confidence you are doing the right things for the business and for them — a critical component of trust. You've asked them what is most important to their satisfaction, performance and productivity. As a result, you have the best chance of setting up a trusting environment if you act immediately on their candid feedback and concerns. This is an easy, effective win for everyone. It shows you've heard them and you care. Not to mention that it reduces risk, ensures regulatory compliance, provides cost savings and increases employee productivity. This one feels like a win-win-win-win-win to us and is why we chose it as a Day 1 priority. We would love to hear your questions."

Around the table, there were a few general questions and observations. Hal told us they had already ordered and received the hardware necessary, and his tech group was ready to do the installation along with the required security systems and network switches. Karen, our head of communications, had already drafted employee communications and passed them to our project management team. Thanking the ABC employees for sharing the Wi-Fi bandwidth concerns and an announcement about the upgrades featured prominently in her message.

In that moment, I began to understand why Jacob felt so strongly about this process. There was so much to learn, I doubted I would ever have enough breadth of knowledge to tackle something like this on my own. I also felt something else: for the first time, true gratitude and appreciation for my PMO team and pride in the work we were doing together.

CHAPTER 16

When Success Equals Succession

MY TEAM HAD THE GOOD FORTUNE TO BE SELECTED TO WORK with the senior leadership team of a highly regarded specialty marketing company — a boutique firm with a long history of satisfied, high-caliber clients. The two founders were well into their 60s and looking forward to retirement. They reached out after three previously failed attempts at selling their business, hoping with help they would be able to make a successful third run at an exit.

Together, we dissected the current state of the organization and the experiences of the prior efforts at selling the organization. A singular, glaring concern became obvious: The two founders referred to their business model, unflatteringly, as "eat what you kill." Each of them was responsible for identifying target business opportunities, working directly and independently with their respective clients and maintaining individual business relationships. Despite their 11-year history together, they had delegated very little authority to their small support team and had no central repository of knowledge about the work they were engaged in and no documented standards or practices.

The critical flaw was simple: Neither had a successor. The business itself was extremely profitable, yet the owners had taken annual distributions and paid lucrative bonuses to staff but not invested in growing infrastructure or the team. There was no one capable of taking their places. The previous attempts at marketing the business had failed because without the founders, there was no business.

Over 22 months, we worked with the team to retain and train talent, document internal processes and procedures, redistribute roles and responsibilities, and put intellectual property protections in place. The founders agreed to invest in bringing in a head of account management and business development to ensure a robust sales pipeline and client relationship continuity, well in advance of their eventual retirement. We partnered with legal and financial experts to accurately value and strategically market the business.

The focus was on finding a strategic acquirer with internal talent to buy the business, rather than a financial buyer who would probably need the owners to stay on for an extended period to grow and manage day-to-day operations. By the time management meetings with potential buyers were taking place, the team had grown the sales pipeline by 62% over the previous year, turnover was at 0% and all bids for the business were at least 100% higher than previous offers.

The founders were able to sell to their top-choice strategic partner — a company with which they had a long-standing vendor-supplier relationship. Along the way, they developed a strong internal succession plan, increased business value, and were able to clearly articulate the near- and long-term transition plans for the owners. The buyers were confident the necessary talent, intellectual property protections and knowledge transfer processes were in place to maintain client satisfaction levels while growing the business, even as the founders exited the organization.

CHAPTER 17

The Cost of Losing Susan

My colleague Kyle also shared this story with me. He was new to his general manager position at the time and was working with a new team, just following the company's first-ever acquisition.

I HEARD A KNOCK ON MY OFFICE DOOR AND LOOKED UP from the spreadsheet I had been working on to see Susan standing in my doorway. "Susan, great to see you, how are you settling into your new role?" Susan looked uncomfortable, shifted her weight and tried to smile. I sensed that something was off, so I invited her to sit down and asked how I could help.

Susan took a deep breath and told me how much she loved her new team members and how helpful they had been as she tried to learn the new production planning software and find ways to navigate some of the quirks in the department. She told me how important it had been for her to participate in the special on-boarding course created to help the new teams come together. She was excited to learn about our history and values, and felt inspired by the vision of the newly combined organization.

I thought it strange that she didn't mention Roger, her new manager, so I asked, "How are things with Roger? Are you getting along well?" Susan looked at the floor and took a very long breath. "He's taking a little getting used to. He's very different from anyone else I've ever worked with, and I'm sure it will just take me some time to make the switch," she said.

Roger was eccentric. He started every conversation with a lesson in word origins. In the beginning, it was interesting, but over time, it grew tiresome and frustrating. He was widely regarded as a key member of the site leadership team and a favorite of the company's CEO. Roger was credited with many improvements in our data analytics and had improved production scheduling and inventory management.

Susan was new. She joined us as part of the ABC Pharma acquisition and was clearly a valuable member of the team. Quiet and reserved, she was intelligent, witty and extremely collaborative. Not only was she a technology wizard, but she had grown up in supply chain planning. She was able to spot issues at a detail level and then see the big, systems-wide impacts. Even more importantly, she could explain them to the people around her in ways they could easily understand and work together to address. ABC rightly, in my opinion, viewed her as high-potential talent. My biggest question was how best to use and continue to develop her skills.

I asked her for more detail about her relationship with Roger. She hesitated and then finally blurted out, "It would be better if he didn't refer to us as oxen and draft horses, all yoked together to pull the organization along. To be honest, I was having a rough day to begin with and his 'inspirational speech' on our first official day together rattled me. I'll continue to give this a shot, but I'm not really sure this is the place for me. That's why I stopped by."

I was caught short. I needed to wrap my head around it and wanted to help. "Have you spoken to anyone else about your concerns?" I asked. "Not yet," she replied. I asked if it would be all right for me to take a few days to do some follow-up and get back to her. She agreed, and we put time on the calendar for early the next week to regroup. How much would it cost, I wondered, if we were to lose Susan?

Her base salary was about $150,000; she was bonus-eligible and part of the company's high-potential development program, so she also received long-term incentives. Employee benefits were about 20% of her salary each year. She had received stellar performance appraisals for the past three years, earning her meaningful salary increases each year, which I expected would continue. The labor market for her skills was very tight and she had unique skills and knowledge of ABC Pharma's legacy IT system, a technology we were obligated to maintain for at least three years after the acquisition. At this point, we were only weeks into that transition period. At a minimum, it would take 60 days to fill her position and then we would have to train the new person. I imagined it would be at least another three months after hiring before a new person in the role was really up to speed.

Using a tool provided by our talent acquisition team (see Appendix C for step calculation of turnover costs), I estimated the actual costs to be around $80,000, although I knew this still did not accurately reflect all the impact of Susan leaving. Her prior department head told me how vital she had been in building his team and how ABC Pharma had invested in additional training and development for her. They hoped, someday, she would be his successor so he could advance his own career, which made Susan a logical successor to Roger. I had to do something to keep her. It was time for me to spend some time with Roger and the rest of his team, and I needed help from our human capital team to do it.

Fast-forward a few months and we were able to address some of Roger's behavioral quirks and learned he much preferred to be in a subject-matter expert role. He had accepted the promotion to manager years ago, at the CEO's request, believing this was the only way to advance his career. It took us a bit to work through the details; ultimately, we were able to promote Susan into the department lead position and, collaborating with Susan and Roger, crafted a technical lead position with no direct reports where Roger could do his best work in progressing our data analytics capabilities and continuously improving our reporting. Another win for everyone!

CHAPTER 18

The Most-Important Employees

NOT LONG AGO, I HAD THE PRIVILEGE OF WORKING WITH A privately owned pharmaceutical company on the first acquisition in their 97-year history. The acquisition would double the size of their business, expand their operating footprint to two states, and triple their product portfolio with significant room for growth and expansion. As a family-owned business with personal funding at stake, a great deal was riding on the success of this transaction. Luckily, the company president and his chief integration officer (CIO), although new to the business, were veteran dealmakers. They reached out to me early in the process and asked for assistance with making sure the right people-decisions were being made. One of their greatest concerns was employee retention.

The acquisition consisted of a single manufacturing facility, which was being carved off from a very large global corporation. Many of the employees had been with the organization for their entire careers and some were being offered competing roles with the parent company. "How will we know who is essential to the business, and what will we do to entice them to stay?" president and CIO asked.

We don't often have complete access to an employee population before closing a deal, but in this case, all of the employees were aware of the pending sale of their facility and the sellers were willing to allow me to speak with the managers and supervisors. My team and I were able to meet with about 20% of the site's workforce. Overall, we held 19 meetings in a week and a half, primarily with team leads, supervisors, managers and directors.

Meetings were conducted with groups of no fewer than three participants, and no meeting included members of a work unit or team who
reported to one another. Most groups were made up of employees from a
variety of departments or workgroups to ensure diverse viewpoints and a
cross-section of functions and skills. Each group was asked the same set of
questions in the same order; however, we allowed the conversations in each
meeting to move naturally and probed for specific details and additional
information where it felt important to capture a more-complete story.

Each group was asked to describe the strongest aspects of their work
as an organization; where they had achieved their greatest successes; what
elements of their environment contributed most significantly to their long
history of accomplishment; and who their most valuable team members
were. Not one interview participant identified themselves, individually, as
critical to the success of the organization. They did, however, identify the
mechanics and maintenance technicians (this site called them EMTs) as
the most-important employees in the plant. These employees were universally identified as being the most-critical staff members for ensuring business continuity and successful manufacturing operation.

We wanted to know more about the EMTs, so we asked each group
to describe the need for and value created by the people in these roles. We
learned the average length of service for an EMT was 25 years. In total, this
team supported more than a dozen manufacturing and packaging machines
in the building. Every one of these machines was more than two dozen
years old, and two of them were more than 35 years old. Of these machines,
only one was designed and built by an organization still in business. There
are no providers of factory repairs left, and few if any options for purchas-
ing aftermarket replacement parts.

Over the years, the EMTs had been able to cobble together machin-
ing equipment, including drill presses and lathes. They built relationships
with local sheet metal vendors, and taught themselves and any newcomers

how to fabricate spare parts and maintain this equipment all on their own, using an old garage on the facility premises.

On average, the EMTs' hard work kept these machines manufacturing and packaging more than 1 billion doses of medication per year, at an average retail value of 20 cents/per dose. Each of the EMTs earned about $42,000 per year plus a site-based performance bonus of approximately 8 percent. The risks to business continuity if any of these EMTs were to leave was enormous, and we needed to convey these risks to the buyer, along with a retention solution.

During our time with the staff, we heard compelling stories of collaboration, survival and flourishing against all odds. They shared a 30-year history of coming together to prove their worth as troubleshooters and creative problem-solvers for a global operating network. There was a great deal of shared history and respect for one another; they told a story of unity and esprit de corps.

In our experience, typical retention plans are designed to hold onto a select few key employees in high-level critical positions. What we learned, through our conversations, shifted our view about what was most important for this site. Our recommendation was to adopt a unique retention mechanism. The integration and operations teams together developed a robust approach with very well-defined integration and post-closing production plans for the site.

Rather than individual retention bonuses, we suggested the aggressive operational objectives be shared with the entire team and used to establish a site-wide performance bonus program. The bonus structure supported the collaborative and cohesive culture of this team and provided clear line of sight to the short-, medium- and long-term outcomes expected of the entire workforce. We were concerned that using a typical key employee retention program would fracture the organization and send a clear message that the "magic" that had kept this team functioning, despite all their historical adversity, was unimportant to the acquirer and would be more likely to cause harm rather than do good.

Appendix C includes an analysis of this situation I produced in collaboration with Jeff Higgins, CEO of the HCMI. In it, you will see a hypothetical Base Year NET ROI $ cost to the business of $3.94M (a low-impact scenario) attributable to the elimination (or loss) of one EMT position. Indeed, the stakes were very high.

The buyer chose to offer the site-wide bonus program instead of individual retention incentives, and their first-year operating results were very positive:

- At three months post-close, they had reduced historic backorder levels from 40% to 0%, experienced 99% employee retention levels and increased their manufacturing production yield to 120% of target.

- At seven months post-close, they had maintained a 99% employee retention rate and their 0% backorder levels, and ended the calendar/fiscal year at +7% to the year-end financial targets.

- At 12 months post-close, they were $2 million over their first 12-month financial projections and the employee engagement survey results showed employees were confident the new leaders would guide them to a positive future.

A Final Thought

"This Machine," by Bill D'Agostino, was commissioned by Laura Queen and a team of collaborators for a stage performance depicting real-life impacts, both human and economic, stemming from mergers and acquisitions activities. The original stage production was produced by Juniper Productions, 29Bison and Homeward Bound at the National Liberty Museum in Philadelphia in January 2019 as part of The NewROI Experience.

THIS MACHINE[124]

By Bill D'Agostino

TAMARA

I know this machine. I know this machine. I know this machine.

Like a lover, like a baby, like the layout of my childhood home.

This machine and me. Seven–eight hours a day for 32 years. I'll come in on weekends if the need arises.

My hands shake outside of this place, but in here they are steady, they are solid, they are sure.

It's just a machine. It's nothing but steel and oil and plastic.

There are few things in life so certain as this: It breaks; I fix it.

It breaks. I fix it. It breaks. I fix it.

Then it runs. Then we run.

I know this machine. I know this machine. I am this machine.
The 20th century was the time of machines, for better or worse. We made things go faster, get bigger.

Now we are in the digital age. They make things smaller. Quicker.
Doubling every two years.

I guess. I don't really understand computers. My grandson tries to teach me.

YouTube. Facebook. Snapchat. Whatsapp. Fucksit.

I don't really understand, but my grandson lives in Minnesota and I like to see his smile on Sundays.

(Hashtag Sunday Smiles.)

So yes, we are in the age of digital.

But these machines are still around. And I am still around.

I am a leftover part.

I know this machine. I am this machine. I am this machine.
My wife says I come home smelling like this machine.

My fingers are raw and rough in all the places I touch it.

I spent two weeks in the hospital in 1994 when this machine acted up and sliced into my leg.

(A lovers' quarrel, you might say.)

I met my wife in the hospital. The machine takes. The machine gives.

Takes. Gives. Takes. Gives.

I am being offered a buyout.

Buy. Out. Buy. Out.

Take. Give. Take? Give?

My wife says I should take it. (Maybe she's jealous?)

My ex-husband says I should take it. (Yes, we are still friends. Life is complicated like that sometimes.)

My grandson loves to build. Legos. Bristle blocks. Doesn't matter. Sculptures of socks and underpants.

He wants to build a machine someday. Bigger. Taller. Faster.

Not smaller. Not quicker.

I am proud. You build a machine, you fix a machine, something gets better.

It may feel silly. To be proud of a machine.

But I am. I hope he will be too.

I am this machine. I am this machine. I am this machine.
I am the only one who knows how to fix this machine.

It is, as they say (no one says this), Un-Google-able. Un-Bing-able. Unknowable. Except by me.

The knowledge of this machine is in my hands. My steady hands.

(No one knows this. No one asked me.)

I like cheese. This is a thing about me. Brie. Cheddar. Gouda. *Gruyere.*
There is good cheese in Wisconsin. Wisconsin is close to Minnesota.

There is one thing better than Hashtag Sunday Smiles. Sunday snuggles.

I will take the buyout. The machine and I will part.

It will break. I won't fix it. We won't run.

I am not a machine. I am not a machine. I am not a machine.

APPENDICES

APPENDIX A

Blended Standards Measures and Metrics

DIGNITY AND EQUALITY METRICS AND DISCLOSURES

Core metrics and disclosures for dignity and inclusion include:

- Diversity and Inclusion Percent

- Pay Equality Percent

- Wage Level Percent

- Risk for human rights violations and incidents of child, forced or compulsory labor

Expanded metrics and disclosures for dignity and inclusion include:

- Pay Gap (percent and ratio)

- Discrimination and harassment

- Freedom of association

- Living wage

CORE METRIC: DIVERSITY AND INCLUSION PERCENT

This is defined as the percentage of employees per employee category by age group, gender and other indicators of diversity (e.g., ethnicity).

Diversity of governance bodies and employees (GRI Disclosure 405-1b)[125]

Percentage of employees per employee category in each of the following diversity categories:

    i.   *Gender;*

    ii. *Age group: under 30 years old, 30–50 years old, over 50 years old;*

    iii. *Other indicators of diversity where relevant (such as minority or vulnerable groups)*

ISO 30414: 4.7.4 — Diversity, 1a Age[126]

Age should include the category 0–14 years [confirmation that no child labour (below 15 years) exists]. A further age categorization can be defined by the organization itself (see table). Within age diversity, reporting metrics should also differentiate between important (strategic) workforce segments; for example, between management and employees, different geographic regions and different organizational functions. The chart below is the ISO 30414 recommended way to display these data.

Employees by age group Years	2020 %	2019 %	2018 %
0–14	0.00	0.00	0.00
15–25	15.3	12.2	11.9
26–39	39.1	41.3	44,7
40–65	39.2	38.6	36.3
65+	6.5	7.9	7.1

ISO 30414: 4.7.4 — Diversity, 1b Gender[127]

To calculate the respective gender in an organization, the following metric can be used:

$$\text{\% of respective gender in an organization} =. \frac{\text{number of respective gender employees}}{\text{Total number of employees}} \times 100$$

ISO 30414 Example for reporting on gender diversity

Employees by gender	2020 %	2019 %	2018 %
Female	32.6	33.8	33.4
Male	63.6	63.5	64.1
Other (non-binary)	3.8	2.7	2.5

ISO 30414: 4.7.4 — Diversity, 1c Disability[128]

According to the International Classification of Functioning, Disability and Health (ICF), disability is an *"umbrella term for impairments, activity limitations and participation restrictions."*[129] The aim of this metric is to display the proportion of disabled members of a workforce as a percentage. The proportion of employees with disabilities is to be determined by dividing the number of disabled people by the total number of employees of an organization.

ISO 30414: 4.7.4 — Diversity, 1d Other indicators of diversity[130]

These indicators include other categories of diversity where relevant, such as race, ethnicity, color, religion or religious belief, status as a military veteran, nationality, sexual orientation, job families, employment tenure. These may be expressed as percentages or ratios, as provided in the examples above.

ISO 30414: 4.7.4 — Diversity, 2 Diversity of leadership and management team(s)[131]

Diversity of leadership/management team with respect to, for example, gender, age, disability and other factors (recommended for internal and external reporting by larger organizations). This measure should also include board member diversity.

CORE METRIC: PAY EQUALITY PERCENT

This measure addresses pay policies and practices, seeking to ensure that they are equitable and transparent, people are paid in accordance with the value of their work, and diversity dimension-related pay gaps are evaluated and addressed. A basic measure of equity is the ratio of basic salary and remuneration for each employee category by significant locations of operation for priority areas of equality: women to men, minor to major ethnic groups, and other relevant equality areas.

Ratio of basic salary and remuneration of women to men (GRI Disclosure 405-2; ISO 30415: 8.6.2.3)[132] [133]

Reporting organizations should report the following information:

    a.   *Ratio of the basic salary and remuneration of women to men for each employee category, by significant location of operation.*

    b.   *The definition used for "significant locations of operation."*

Reporting recommendations: When compiling the information specified in GRI Disclosure 405-2, the reporting organization should base remuneration on the average pay of each gender grouping within each employee category.

CORE METRIC: WAGE LEVEL PERCENT

These measures aim to establish transparence in wage/earnings equality or inequality. The measures look at pay ratios, including CEO to workers, entry wage by genders (and other diversity measures) and the local minimum wage. While the WEF/IBC guidelines and GRI standards address gender-related equity only, we argue that these same metrics should be used to look at other employee categories as well (e.g., race, nationality, sexual orientation, veteran status, disability, etc.).

Ratios of standard entry level wage by gender compared to local minimum wage (GRI Disclosure 202-1; ISO 30415: 8.6.3.1, 8.6.3.2)[134] [135]

Reporting organizations should report the following information:

a. *When a significant proportion of employees are compensated based on wages subject to minimum wage rules, report the relevant ratio of the entry-level wage by gender at significant locations of operation to the minimum wage.*

b. *When a significant proportion of other workers (excluding employees) performing the organization's activities are compensated based on wages subject to minimum wage rules, describe the actions taken to determine whether these workers are paid above the minimum wage.*

c. *Whether a local minimum wage is absent or variable at significant locations of operation, by gender. In circumstances in which different minimums can be used as a reference, report which minimum wage is being used.*

d. *The definition used for "significant locations of operation."*

Ratio of CEO compensation to employees

Provide a ratio, expressed as both ratio and percent, of the annual total compensation of the CEO to the median of the annual total compensation of all its employees except the CEO.

CORE METRIC: RISK FOR HUMAN RIGHT VIOLATIONS AND INCIDENTS OF CHILD, FORCED OR COMPULSORY LABOR

In the UN SDGs, the world committed to ending all forms of child labor by 2025. The International Labour Organization (ILO) reports 94 million fewer children in child labor in the past two decades, but in times of economic crisis and social disruption, these accomplishments are in jeopardy.[136] These measures seek transparency and awareness of child and other forms of compulsory labor practices, such as slave or bonded labor, as a way to continue the hard-won progress toward this global sustainability commitment. The WEF/IBC measures include:

Operations and suppliers at significant risk for incidents of child labor (GRI Disclosure 408-1b, 409-1a)[137] [138]

Operations and suppliers considered to have significant risk for incidents of child, forced or compulsory labor. Such risks could emerge in relation to:

    a. *Type of operation (such as manufacturing plant) and type of supplier; and*

    b. *Countries or geographic areas with operations and suppliers considered at risk.*

Human rights review, grievance impact and modern slavery (number and percent) (Expanded Metric)

Organizations choosing to disclose expanded metrics should include the details below in addition to the incidents of child labor metrics, above.

    a. *Total number and percentage of operations that have been subject to human rights reviews or human rights impact assessments, by country.*

b. *Number and type of grievances reported with associated impact related to a salient human rights issue in the reporting period and an explanation of type of impacts.*

c. *Number and percentage of operations and suppliers considered to have a significant risk for incidents of child, forced or compulsory labour. Such risks could emerge in relation to:*

   i. *Type of operation (such as manufacturing plant) and type of supplier; and*

   ii. *Countries or geographic areas with operations suppliers considered at risk.*

EXPANDED METRIC: PAY GAP (PERCENT AND RATIO)

These measures seek to ensure transparency of equitable pay practices at substantially more granular levels than the core measures. They include:

Ratio of average salary and remuneration (ISO 30414: 4.7.3 - Costs (3)) [139]

Mean pay gap of basic salary and remuneration of full-time relevant employees based on gender (women to men) and indicators of diversity (e.g., Black, Asian, Minority Ethnic (BAME) to non-BAME) at a company level or by significant location of operation. Measurements are:

The average salary and remuneration within identified categories of the workforce defined by the organization reported as a ratio based on FTE.

$$\text{Ratio of avg. salary and remuneration} = \frac{\text{Ratio of avg. total comp. of all employees}}{\text{Annual total comp. of defined categories or individuals}}$$

Where comp. = compensation

NOTE: Defined categories or individuals include, for example, the most senior executives in the organization, or specific categories (e.g., BAME).

Annual total compensation ratio (GRI 102-38)[140]

Ratio of the annual total compensation for the organization's highest-paid individual in each country of significant operations to the median annual total compensation for all employees (excluding the highest-paid individual) in the same country. Organizations should report the following information:

Ratio of the annual total compensation for the organization's highest-paid individual in each country [or] significant operation to the median annual total compensation for all employees (excluding the highest-paid individual) in the same country [or operation].

When compiling the information specified in Disclosure 102-38, the reporting organization shall, for each country [or] significant operation:

a. *Identify the highest-paid individual for the reporting period as defined by total compensation;*

b. *Calculate the median annual total compensation for all employees, except the highest-paid individual;*

c. *Calculate the ratio of the annual total compensation for the highest-paid individual to the median annual total compensation for all employees.*

EXPANDED METRIC: DISCRIMINATION AND HARASSMENT

Discrimination and harassment incidents (number) and the total amount of monetary losses ($) (GRI 406-1, Adapted from SASB FR-310a.4; ISO 30414 4.7.2 (1))[141] [142]

Number of discrimination and harassment incidents, status of the incidents and actions taken, and total amount of monetary losses as a result of legal proceedings associated with violations of law and employment discrimination. Organizations should report the following information:

- *Total number of incidents of discrimination during the reporting period.*

- *Status of the incidents and actions taken with reference to the following:*

    a. *Incident reviewed by the organization;*

    b. *Remediation plans being implemented;*

    c. *Remediation plans that have been implemented, with results reviewed through routine internal management review processes;*

    d. *Incident no longer subject to action.*

When compiling the information specified in [this measure], the reporting organization shall include incidents of discrimination on the grounds of race, color, gender, sexual orientation, religion, political opinion, national [origin], or social origin (as defined by the ILO), or other relevant forms of discrimination involving internal and/or external stakeholders in all operations in the reporting period.

EXPANDED METRIC: FREEDOM OF ASSOCIATION

Freedom of association and collective bargaining at risk (percent) (GRI Disclosure 407-1, 29 U.S.C. §§ 151-169)[143] [144]

Percentage of active workforce covered under collective bargaining agreements and an explanation of the evaluation conducted on suppliers for which the right to freedom of association and collective bargaining is at risk, including measures taken by the organization to address this risk. Reporting organizations should report the following information:

    a. *Operations and suppliers in which workers' rights to exercise freedom of association or collective bargaining may be violated or at significant risk either in terms of:*

        i. *Type of operation (such as manufacturing plant) and supplier;*

        ii. *Countries of geographic areas with operations and suppliers considered at risk*

    b. *Measures taken by the organization in the reporting period intended to support rights to exercise freedom of association and collective bargaining.*

EXPANDED METRIC: LIVING WAGE

Living wage (percent) (MIT Living Wage Calculator, EPIC)[145] [146]

This measure looks at current wages against the living wage for employees and contractors in states and localities where the company is operating. The Living Wage Calculator was first created in 2004 by Dr. Amy K. Glasmeier. "*The living wage is the minimum income standards that, if met, draws a very fine line between the financial independence of the working poor and the need to seek our public assistance or suffer consistent and severe housing and food insecurity. In light of this fact, the living wage is perhaps better defined as a minimum subsistence wage for persons living in the United States. The living wage model generates a cost of living estimate that exceeds the federal poverty thresholds. As calculated, the living wage estimate accounts for the basic needs of a family. The living wage model does not include funds that cover what many may consider as necessities enjoyed by many Americans. The tool does not include funds for pre-prepared meals or those eating in restaurants. [The model does] not add funds for entertainment, nor [does it] incorporate leisure time for unpaid vacation or holidays. Lastly, the calculated living wage does not provide a financial means to enable savings and investment for the purchase of capital assets (e.g., provisions for retirement or home purchases)."*

Reporting organizations may access and use the Living Wage Calculator for free here:

https://livingwage.mit.edu.

This chart summarizes the core and expanded metrics, metric descriptions and relationship to specific guidelines.

People Pillar: Dignity and Equality Core Metrics and disclosures[147]			
Core Metric/Disclosure	Description	WEF Metric/Measure and Recommendation	ISO or other HR metrics
Diversity and Inclusion %	Percentage of employees per employee category, by age group, gender and other indicator of diversity (e.g., ethnicity) *WEF/IBC*	GRI 405-1b	ISO 30414 4.7.4 Diversity

Pay Equality %	Ratio of basic salary and remuneration for each employee category by significant locations of operation for priority areas of equality: women to men, minor to major ethnic groups, and other relevant equality areas. *WEF/IBC*	Adapted from GRI 405-2	ISO 30415 8.6.3.1, 8.6.3.2
Wage Level Percent	Ratios of standard entry level wage by gender compared to local minimum wage, *and* ratio of total annual compensation of the CEO to median of annual total compensation of all its employees except the CEO.	GRI 202-1, Adapted from Dodd-Frank Act, US SEC Regulations	ISO 30415 8.6.3.1, 8.6.3.2
Risks for incidents of child, forced and compulsory labor	An explanation of the operations and suppliers considered to have significant risk for incidents of child, forced or compulsory labor.	GRI 408-1b, GRI 409-1a	

People Pillar: Dignity and Equality Expanded Metrics and Disclosures			
Pay Gap (percent and ratio)	Mean pay gap of basic salary and remuneration of full-time relevant employees based on categories of diversity and ratio of annual total compensation to organization's highest paid employees by location.	Adapted from UK Government guidance on gender and ethnicity pay gap reporting GRI 102-38	ISO 30415 8.6.3.1, 8.6.3.2, 8.6.3.3
Discrimination and harassment incidents (number) and the total amount of monetary losses (costs)	Number of discrimination and harassment incidents, status and amount of monetary losses.	GRI 406-1, Adapted from SASB FR-310a.4	ISO 30414 4.7.2 Compliance and ethics (1), ISO 30415 7.3.5
Freedom of association and collective bargaining at risk (percent)	Percentage of active workforce covered under collective bargaining agreements and assessment of right to freedom of association and collective bargaining for suppliers	SASB CN0401-17, GRI 407-1, WDI 7.2	NATIONAL LABOR RELATIONS ACT Also cited NLRA or the Act; 29 U.S.C. §§ 151-169 [Title 29, Chapter 7, Subchapter II, United States Code]

Human rights review, grievance impact and modern slavery (number and percent)	Number and percent of operations subject to human rights reviews; number and type of human rights grievances; number and percentage of operations and suppliers considered at risk for human rights risks	GRI 412-1, UN Guiding Principles, GRI 408-1a, Adapted from GRI-408-1a and GRI 409-1, WDI 7.5	None
Living wage (percent)	Current wages against the living wage for employees in states and localities where the company is operating.	MIT Living Wage Tool, EPIC	ISO 30415 8.6.3.1, 8.6.3.2

HEALTH AND WELL-BEING CORE METRICS AND DISCLOSURES

Health and Safety Percent

In many places, including the United States, occupational health and safety are shaped by the law. ISO 30414 argues that "promoting health, safety and well-being and the prevention of work-related accidents and illnesses relies on documented risk assessments and hazard identification ... [including] the timely reporting of work or occupations-related accidents, fatalities, injuries, disease and illness." Accordingly, these measures require that reporting organizations disclose:

- *The number and rate of fatalities as a result of work-related injury; high-consequence work-related injuries (excluding fatalities); recordable work-related injuries; main types of work-related injury; and the number of hours worked.*

- *An explanation of how the organization facilitates workers' access to non-occupational medical and healthcare services, and the scope of access provided for employees and workers.*

These data provide information about an organization's prioritization of and investment in employees' health and well-being. Doing so ensures that the workplace protects employees from harm, prevents ill-health, supports business continuity, promotes organizational productivity and efficiency and takes care to limit negative impacts to our wider society.

Organizational health, safety and well-being (ISO 30414 4.7.7)[148]

The following metrics are recommended by ISO and required by the United States Occupational Safety and Health Administration (OSHA).

Lost time for work-related injuries, accidents and disease (ISO 30414 4.7.7 — Organizational health, safety and well-being (1))[149]

Lost time for injuries* (days or hours) = $\dfrac{\text{Amount of working time lost due to accidents at work in a given period of time}}{\text{Total amount of expected work time in a given work period}}$

Note: includes time lost for work-related illness and disease

Number of occupational accidents (recordable incidents) (ISO 30414 4.7.7 — Organizational health, safety and well-being (2))[150]

This metric includes accidents that occur in the course of employment and are caused by the hazards related to such work. OSHA defines recordable incidents as:

- *Any work-related fatality*

- *Any work-related injury or illness that results in loss of consciousness, days away from work, restricted work or transfer to another job*

- *Any work-related injury or illness requiring medical treatment beyond first aid*

- *Any work-related diagnosed case of cancer, chronic irreversible diseases, fractured or cracked bones or teeth, and punctured eardrums*

- *There are special recording criteria for work-related cases involving needlesticks and sharps injuries; medical removal, hearing loss, and tuberculosis.*

This metric is often reported as the number of occupational accidents meeting the definitions above and as a rate of accidents in 1 million work hours (see below).

$$Accident\ rate = \frac{Sum\ of\ occupational\ accidents\ in\ a\ given\ time\ period}{Employee\ work\ hours\ in\ a\ given\ time\ period} \times 1{,}000{,}000\ hours$$

Workers covered by an occupational health and safety management system (GRI 403-9)[151]

The WEF/IBC framework suggests using GRI: 403-9a&b as the reporting standard. This book is intended primarily for U.S.-centric organizations, therefore, we recommend using the OSHA/ISO reporting standards (above) and adding the following reporting requirements, which refer reporting organizations to the federally mandated reporting requirements of OSHA 29 CFR 1904.[152] Reporting organizations shall report the following information.

a. *If the organization has implemented an occupational health and safety management system based on legal requirements and/or recognized standards/guidelines:*

    i. *The number and percentage of all employees and workers who are not employees but whose work and/or workplace is controlled by the organizations, which are covered by such a system;*

    ii. *The number and percentage of all employees and workers who are not employees but whose work and/or workplace is controlled by the organization, which is covered by such a system that has been internally audited;*

    iii. *The number and percentage of all employees and workers who are not employees but who work and/or workplace is controlled by the organization, which is covered by such a system that has been audited or certified by an external party.*

b. *Whether and if so, why, any workers have been excluded for this disclosure, including the types of worker excluded.*

c. *Any contextual information necessary to understand how the data have been compiled, such as any standards, methodologies and assumptions used.*

Promotion of worker health (GRI 403-6)[153]

Reporting organizations should report the following information for employees and for workers who are not employees but whose work and/or workplace is controlled by the organization:

a. *An explanation of how the organization facilitates workers' access to non-occupational medical and healthcare services, and the scope of access provided.*

b. *A description of any voluntary health promotion services and programs offered to workers to address major non-work-related health risks, including the specific health risks addressed and how the organization facilitates workers' access to these services or programs.*

HEALTH AND WELL-BEING EXPANDED METRICS AND DISCLOSURES

Monetized impacts of work-related incidents on organization (number and costs) (Access Economics P/L 2004 and European Commission)[154]

This metric looks at the economic impacts of work-related injuries and illnesses and their direct costs to employees or employers per incident (including actions and/or fines from regulators, property damage, healthcare costs, compensation costs to the employees).

Number of people killed during work (ISO 30414 4.7.7 — Organizational health, safety and well-being (3))[155]

These metrics measure the number of people killed during work (fatalities, deaths, mortality rate) due to accidents or illnesses in a given time-period (e.g., a year). Reporting organizations should report the following information:

a. *For all employees:*

i. *The number of fatalities as a result of work-related ill health;*

ii. *The number of cases of recordable work-related ill health;*

     iii. *The main types of work-related ill health.*

  b. *For all workers who are not employees but whose work and/or workplace is controlled by the organizations:*

     i. *The number of fatalities as a result of work-related ill health;*

     ii. *The number of cases of recordable work-related ill health;*

     iii. *The main types of work-related ill health.*

The rate of work-related fatalities *may be measured as follows:*

$$\text{Fatality rate} = \frac{\textit{Number of fatal occupational injuries}}{\textit{Total number of employees}}$$

Hazard identification, risk assessment and incident identification (GRI Disclosure 403-2a)[156]

Organizations should report the following information for employees and for workers who are not employees but whose work and/or workplace is controlled by the organization:

A description of the processes used to identify work-related hazards and assess risks on a routine and non-routine basis, and to apply the hierarchy of controls to eliminate hazards and minimize risks, including:

  a. *How the organization ensures the quality of these processes, including the competency of those who carry them out;*

  b. *How the results of these processes are used to evaluate and continually improve the occupations health and safety management system.*

Workforce availability — Absenteeism (ISO 30414: 4.7.12 (4))[157]

Absenteeism is a measure of workforce availability, sometimes measured as a liability, and looks at total workforce availability minus planned and unplanned leave. Absences include time away from work because of sickness, injury, medical leaves, personal issues, strikes or work protests, or willful absence such as job dissatisfaction. Vacation, statutory holidays, company-sanctioned events and authorized leaves are not included in the absenteeism-rate calculation.

$$\text{Absenteeism rate} = \frac{\textit{Number of absent days}}{\textit{Number of available work-days in a given time period}}$$

People Pillar: Health and Well-Being Core Metrics[158]			
	Description	**WEF/IBC Metric Recommendation**	**ISO or Other HR metrics**
Health and Safety Percent	Number of work-related fatalities, illnesses and injuries and an explanation of how the organization facilitates workers' access to non-occupational medical and healthcare services.	GRI:2018 403–9a&b GRI:2018 403–6a	GRI: 2018 403-8 ISO 4.7.7 (1&2) OSHA Record-keeping: 29 CFR 1904
People Pillar: Health and Well-Being Expanded Metrics			
Monetized impacts of work-related incidents on organization (number and costs)	Direct economic costs of work-related injuries and illnesses.	Adapted indicator based on European Commission, Safe Work Australia	None

Employee well-being (number and percent)	Work-related fatalities; employee participation in "best-practice" health and wellness programs; company-wide absenteeism.	GRI:2018 403-10a&b, EPIC, GRI:2016 403-2a	ISO 30414:4.7.7 (3), OSHA Record-keeping: 29 CFR 1904, ISO 30414:4.7.12 (4)

SKILLS FOR THE FUTURE CORE METRICS AND DISCLOSURES

Employees' skills, abilities, performance and productivity are significant components of an organization's competitive advantage. Their process and procedural knowledge and skills are also critical in minimizing risk and ensuring business continuity. Personal development and opportunities for career advancement are also critical components of employee engagement. For these and other reasons, metrics designed to understand the average number of training hours per person by employment level and diversity characteristics in a given period are important. Measuring training, learning outcomes and employer investment in knowledge and skills development is a difficult task. In their 2019 publication *Getting Skills Right: Future-Ready Adult Learning System*s, the OECD argues:

> *There needs to be an equitable sharing of the financing of adult learning in line with ability to pay and the benefits[that] accrue to individuals, firms and societies. [However, a] key challenge going forward will be to improve data collection of financing of adult learning, which is extremely scant at the moment. Factors contributing to this lack of data include: the financing of adult learning by a range of actors; there are no official statistic on adult learning financing as such; accounting practices vary between countries; and there is no commonly agreed definition of adult learning.*"[159]

The following recommended metrics and disclosures are steps in the right direction.

Average hours of training per year per employee (GRI Disclosure 404-1)[160]

Reporting organizations should provide average hours of training that the organization's employees have undertaken during the reporting period, by:

    i.   Gender

    ii. Employee category

$$\text{Average training hours per employee} = \frac{\text{Total number of training hours provided to an employee}}{\text{Total number of employees}}$$

$$\text{Average training hours per female} = \frac{\text{Total number of training hours provided to female employees}}{\text{Total number of female employees}}$$

Leadership development (ISO 30414 4.7.5(3))[161]

These metrics looks at an organization's leadership and asks them to report the:

- *percentage of leaders who have participated in leadership development programs within a defined period;*

- *percentage of leaders who have participated in training.*

Learning and development (ISO 30414 4.7.10 (2))[162]

Looking below the leadership level of an organization, these measures of staff learning and development ask for:

a. Percentage of employees who participate in training compared with total number of employees per year (additionally recommended for internal reporting by subject matter experts (SME) group;

b. Average formalized training hours per employee (additionally recommended for internal reporting by SME group) — average number of hours an organization's people participate in formalized training activities, such as hours of classroom learning or e-learning per employee per year;

c. Percentage of employees who participate in formalized training in different categories (e.g., mandatory training, leadership, sales, communication, IT training, technical subjects, team development, intercultural skills, single/group coaching, mentoring, diversity), listing training subjects per employee.

Total development and training costs (ISO 30414 4.7.10 (1))[163]

These measures look at the investments in development and training for the organization's people with the expectation that these investments provide future benefits, including greater workforce productivity, higher performance, etc.

This metric is defined as the total expenses of an organization for training and development (off-the-job and workplace learning). It includes the total costs per employee of classroom training, e-learning, on-the-job training for their current position and future development steps.

Direct costs of developing and training include teaching materials, fees, charges and similar expenses. Indirect costs should be excluded, such as costs of lost work time.

Average training and development expenditure per employee (WEF/IBC Measuring Stakeholder Capitalism: Skills for the future)[164]

This metric breaks down total investment for employee training and development in a specific period to an average per-employee investment and may be calculated as:

$$\text{Average cost of training per employee} = \frac{\text{Total costs of training and development}}{\text{Total number of employees}}$$

SKILLS FOR THE FUTURE EXPANDED METRICS AND DISCLOSURES

Number of unfilled skilled positions (number and percent) (WBCSD Measuring Impact Framework)[165]

According to the WBCSD Measuring Impact Framework Methodology, "skills and training programs can play a critical role in providing economic opportunities for previously disadvantaged people. As a result, it is important to assess changes in the demographic make-up (e.g., race, age, gender, etc.) of program participants and impacts this may have on social equality in the area of assessment." These measures are qualitative indicators aimed at "understanding the impacts of skills and training programs."

1. *Number (#) of unfilled skilled positions*

2. *Number (#) and percent (%) of "skilled" positions for which the company will hire totally unskilled candidates and train them*

Monetized impacts of training — Increased earning capacity as a result of training intervention (percent and dollars) (OECD: Getting Skills Right: Future Ready Adult Learning Systems)[166]

Reporting organizations should provide:

1. *The amount invested in training as a percentage (%) of payroll*

2. *Effectiveness of the training and development through increased revenue, productivity gains, employee engagement and/or internal hire rates*

   Specific recommended measures include (*ISO 30414 4.7.9 (5, 6, 9)* and Kirkpatrick's Level 4)[167] [168]

   a. Percentage of positions filled internally — an organization's internal recruiting for the reoccupation of vacant positions

   b. Percentage of vacant critical positions filled internally — an organization's internal recruiting for the reoccupation of vacant critical positions

   c. Internal mobility rate (lateral moves, promotions) — number of moves between locations and functions in an organization

   d. Return-on-investment (ROI) of training — measure of gain or business impact from training (e.g., productivity improvement, reduced waste/scrap, sales revenue), or dollar amount returned as a benefit for every dollar spent on training.

$$\text{Training ROI} = \frac{\text{Total Benefit from Training} - \text{Total Costs of Training}}{\text{Total Costs of Training}}$$

People Pillar: Skills for the Future Core Metrics[169]			
	Description	WEF/IBC Metric Recommendation	ISO or other HR metrics
Training provided (number and investment)	Training hours and expenditure per full-time employee	GRI 404-1 SASB HC 101-15	ISO 30414 4.7.10 (2a,b,c) ISO 30414 4.7.5 (3) Kirkpatrick Model: Levels 1-4 ISO 30414 4.7.10 (1)
People Pillar: Skills for the Future Expanded Metrics			
Number of unfilled skilled positions (number and percent)	Number of unfilled skilled positions and % of which skilled positions for which unskilled hires will be made and trained	WBCSD Measuring Impact Framework Methodology v. 1.0 (2008)	
Monetized impacts of training — increased earning capacity as a result of training intervention (percent, wage/salary increase)	Investment in training as a % of payroll and effectiveness of training measured through increased revenue, productivity gains, employee engagement and/or internal hire rates.	Adapted from OECD 27, 28 WDI 5.5	Kirkpatrick Model: Level 4 ISO 30414 4.7.9 (5, 6, 9)

Beyond those included in the WEF/IBC's People Pillar are measures connected to the creation of economic and social prosperity. These measures are tied to UN SDG Goals 1: No Poverty, 8: Decent Work and Economic Growth; 9: Industry, Innovation and Infrastructure; and 10: Reduced Inequalities. This Prosperity Pillar seeks to shed light on company value as "increasingly reflected in off-balance sheet intangible assets and other value drivers associated with economic and social prosperity. Long-term value creation is critical for business performance, competitive advantage, mitigating risk and strengthening stakeholder relationships.

Even when there is not yet a direct link between the SDGs and financial performance, stakeholders have indicated that reporting on these metrics is important for sustainable value creation."[170]

For our purposes, the themes in the Prosperity Pillar most connected to human capital are Employment and Wealth Generation and Community and Social Vitality. Employment and Wealth Generation looks at contributions to the wider society through "job creation and investing in the productive capacity of the economy. Job creation, employee retention and investments in society are key ... [t]these investments contribute to better living standards and wealth creation in the long term. Strong economic prosperity drives a more educated workforce and higher workforce productivity, as well as greater buying power for the company's customer base."[171]

Community and Social Vitality highlights "the critical contribution that companies make to long-term value creation and a healthy, diverse, prosperous society. More equitable and inclusive economies reinforce the social license of businesses to operate, strengthen workforce talent pools, enlarge the customer base and its buying power, and enhance supplier relationships and partnerships in the communities in which companies operate."[172]

I address only those measures in this pillar that are connected directly to human capital within organizations.

EMPLOYMENT AND WEALTH GENERATION METRICS AND DISCLOSURES (HUMAN CAPITAL ONLY)

Absolute number and rate of employment (GRI 401-1a&b)[173]

This measure looks at the total number and rate of new employee hires during the reporting period by age group, gender, and other indicators of diversity and region/location or functional business unit. It also looks at the total number and rate of employee turnover during the reporting period by age group, gender, and other indicators of diversity and region/

location or functional business unit. In both cases, as it relates to issues of employee engagement, this measure might be extended to look at attrition and retention at the manager/supervisor level as well.

Organizations should report the following information:

a. *Total number and rate of new employee hires during the reporting period, by age group, gender and region*

b. *Total number and rate of employee turnover during the reporting period by age group, gender and region*

Turnover rate (ISO 30414 4.7.9 (11))[174]

This metric measures the number of people who leave the organization due to dismissal, attrition and other reasons compared with the total number of people in the organization. It includes all turnover regardless of reason. It is also useful to calculate a separate figure for voluntary turnover (e.g., retirements, resignations) and for involuntary turnover (e.g., redundancies, performance issues), because these can have particularly adverse impact on the business.

$$\text{Turnover rate} = \frac{\text{Total number of leavers over a given period of time}}{\text{Average total number of employees over a given period of time}} \times 100$$

Direct economic value generated and distributed (GRI Disclosure 201-1)[175]

Economic contribution looks at how a company creates or destroys value for stakeholders during a given period of time. Reporting organizations should provide the following information:

a. Direct economic value generated and distributed (EVG&D) on an accrual basis, including the basic components for the organization's global operations as listed below. If data are presented on a cash basis, report the justification for this decision in addition to the following basic components:

i. Direct economic value generated — revenues;

ii. Economic value distributed — operating costs, employee wages and benefits, payments to providers of capital, payments to government by country, and community investments;

iii. Economic value retained — EVG&D minus economic value distributed.

b. Where significant, report EVG&D separately at country, regional or market levels, and the criteria used for defining significance.

Human Capital Value Added (HCVA)

This metric assesses the amount of financial value (profit) an average employee brings to an organization.

$$\text{Human Capital Value Added} = \frac{(\text{Revenue} - (\text{Operating Expenses} - (\text{Payroll} + \text{Benefits})))}{\text{Total Headcount}}$$

Financial assistance received from government [or other entities] (GRI Disclosure 201-4)[176]

This measure looks at government or other entities' contribution to an organization. Organizations should report the following:

a. *Total monetary value of financial assistance received by the organization from any government [or other assistance entity] during the reporting period, including:*

    i. *Tax relief and tax credits;*

    ii. *Subsidies;*

    iii. *Investment grants, research and development grants, and other relevant types of grants [e.g., training, development and learning grants];*

    iv. *Awards;*

    v. *Royalty holidays;*

    vi. *Financial assistance form Export Credit Agencies (ECAs);*

    vii. *Financial incentives;*

    viii. *Other financial benefits received or receivable from any government [or other entity e.g., foundations, academic institutions, etc.] for any operation.*

b. *These [details presented by country, location and/or business unit as applicable].*

c. *Whether, and the extent to which, any government or other granting entity is part of the shareholding structure.*

Prosperity Pillar: Employment and Wealth Generation Core Metrics (Human Capital only)[177]			
	Description	WEF/IBC Metric Recommendation	ISO or other HR metrics
Absolute number and rate of employment	Total number and rate of new employee hires and leavers during the reporting period	Adapted from GRI 401-1a&b	ISO 30414 4.7.9 (11)
Economic Contribution	Direct economic value generated and distributed (EVG&D), on an accrual basis, covering the basic components of business opera-tions — to include wages and benefits	GRI 201-1 GRI 201-4	Human Capital Value Added (HCVA)

Community and Social Vitality Core Metrics and Disclosures (Human Capital only)

Total tax paid and additional tax remitted (WEF/IBC Measuring Stakeholder Capitalism framework)[178]

1. *The total global tax borne by the company, including corporate income taxes, property taxes, property taxes, non-creditable VAT and other sales taxes, employer-paid payroll taxes, and other taxes that constitute costs to the company, by category of taxes.*

2. *The total additional global tax collected by the company on behalf of other taxpayers, including VAT and employee-related taxes that are remitted by the company on behalf of customers or employees, by category of taxes.*

(See EVG&D (*GRI Disclosure 201-1*) for reporting requirements)

Prosperity Pillar: Community and Social Vitality (Human Capital only)[179]			
	Description	WEF/IBC Metric Recommendation	ISO or other HR metrics
Total tax paid	Total global taxes paid, including employer-paid payroll taxes	Adapted from GRI 201-1	None
Prosperity Pillar: Community and Social Vitality (Human Capital only)			
Additional tax remitted	Total additional global tax collected by the company, including employee-related taxes	Adapted from GRI 201-1	None

WHAT'S MISSING

There are many other measures of human capital not contemplated in the WEF/IBC Sustainability Metrics framework. Notably missing include organization-specific measures of investment, performance and productivity, as well as measures of culture and employee engagement. Some of these measures are recommended by other reporting frameworks, including EPIC.[180] Others are considered good management practices and are highly recommended as internal measures of human capital contribution to organizational value creation. The next sections provide details about a few of these missing metrics.

It is worth noting that there are many other metrics and measures. This appendix is not intended to be an exhaustive or authoritative compendium; my hope was to create a level of association and alignment among the current reporting frameworks with the addition of some practical suggestions.

ORGANIZATION-SPECIFIC MEASURES OF PERFORMANCE AND PRODUCTIVITY

In an earlier section, I discussed the importance of company- and unit-specific measures of success: KPIs. Among these are metrics related to financial performance and productivity. Although not included in the WEF/IBC sustainability reporting metrics, these are essential indicators of the value HR departments and employees contribute to organizations.

Human Capital Return on Investment (ROI) (ISO 30414 4.7.8 (2))[181]

This metric shows how effectively the investment in human capital is supporting the organization's goals. HCROI, as it is commonly called, is the amount returned for every dollar spent (e.g., wages, benefits, etc.) on human capital. It shows the ratio of income/revenue to employment costs and is calculated as:

$$HCROI = \frac{Revenue - (Expenses - (Pay + Benefits))}{Pay + Benefits}$$

EBIT/EBITDA/revenue/turnover/profit per employee (ISO 30414 4.7.8 (1))[182]

In for-profit organizations, these measures are used to compare productivity ratios on a per-employee basis. These metrics are used to compare a company's productivity to the market. *These ratios can be used as a simple metric for cost reduction and control or the implementation of a system of performance-based compensation. A historical analysis of this ratio can offer important information about the development of the organization's success with a chosen strategy. This analysis allows value added by employees, depending on the organization's growth, to be monitored. Applicability of those values may differ by context; for example, size, country, age of the organization or business sector* (recall the discussion of materiality).

In accounting and finance, earnings before interest and taxes (EBIT) is a measure of a firm's profit that includes all expenses except interest and income tax expenses. It is a measure of an organization's ability to produce income from its operations in a given time period. This ratio may be calculated as follows:

$$\text{EBIT per employee} = \frac{\text{Revenue - (expenses + interest + taxes)}}{\text{Total number of employees}}$$

Similarly, EBITDA per employee, a measure of profit per employee before depreciation and amortization, may be calculated as:

$$\text{EBITDA per employee} = \frac{\text{Revenues - (expenses + interest + taxes + depreciation + amortization)}}{\text{Total number of employees}}$$

Total costs of workforce (TCOW) (ISO 30414 4.7.3 (1&2))[183]

This metric is a key indicator of the financial value given by an organization to managing, maintaining and developing its workforce. It includes external workforce costs and only the actual amount paid for all workforce wages. TCOW may be calculated as:

TCOW = total compensation costs + benefits costs + external workforce costs *where* **external workforce costs** *include expenses for contractors, consultants, temporary workers and gig workers. It is defined as the sum of external workforce-related expenses; for example temporary worker invoices, agency fees, independent contractor costs and consultant costs.*

Organization-specific measures of performance and productivity			
	Description	WEF/IBC Metric Recommendation	ISO or other HR metrics
Human Capital ROI	Shows how effectively the investment in human capital is supporting organizational goals.	None	ISO 30414 4.7.8 (2)
EBITDA per Employee	Measures the bottom-line financial productivity of the organization as brought about collectively by individual employees.	None	ISO 30414 4.7.8 (1)
Total Costs of Workforce (TCOW)	The value of managing, maintaining and developing and organization's workforce	None	ISO 30414 4.7.3 (1&2) EPIC Workforce Cost

APPENDIX B

Examples of Public Disclosures

Pay Equity Statement

Prudential's Total Rewards is integral to our employee value proposition. This package includes compensation, as well as benefits and talent programs and resources available to our employees.

As part of our annual human resources strategy update, our Board reviews the status of our pay practices and the broad range of our diversity and inclusion efforts.

All roles in our U.S. organization are reviewed against relevant market data. Our Total Rewards and talent programs enable Prudential to recruit and promote talent within the context of an individual's background, experience and performance.

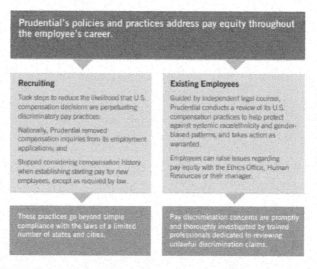

Prudential's policies and practices address pay equity throughout the employee's career.

Recruiting

Took steps to reduce the likelihood that U.S. compensation decisions are perpetuating discriminatory pay practices;

Nationally, Prudential removed compensation inquiries from its employment applications; and

Stopped considering compensation history when establishing starting pay for new employees, except as required by law.

These practices go beyond simple compliance with the laws of a limited number of states and cities.

Existing Employees

Guided by independent legal counsel, Prudential conducts a review of its U.S. compensation practices to help protect against systemic race/ethnicity and gender-biased patterns, and takes action as warranted.

Employees can raise issues regarding pay equity with the Ethics Office, Human Resources or their manager.

Pay discrimination concerns are promptly and thoroughly investigated by trained professionals dedicated to reviewing unlawful discrimination claims.

In addition to this integrated approach that encourages a proactive review of pay equity on an ongoing basis, and that we satisfy our heightened obligations as a federal contractor, we periodically retain independent external experts to conduct pay equity analyses for our U.S. population.

In 2018, salary, bonus and equity were evaluated and the results showed, when accounting for relevant factors including job and location, that women and Asian employees were paid at least 100% of the pay of male and White employees, respectively. Additionally, Black employees were paid at 99.9% and Hispanic employees were paid at 99.4% of the pay of non-Hispanic White employees.

In 2020, salary was evaluated and the results showed, when accounting for relevant factors including job and location, that women and Asian employees were paid at least 100% of the pay of male and White employees, respectively. Additionally, Black employees were paid at 99.0% and Hispanic employees were paid at 98.3% of the pay of non-Hispanic White employees.

 Prudential

184

PRUDENTIAL IS COMMITTED TO THE FUTURE OF WORK

In the U.S. and around the world, employers are struggling to find skilled talent, while many people lack access to proper training to fill open positions.

In America alone, **6 million people were unemployed** as of July 2019 — yet **7.3 million job openings remained unfilled.**

Prudential, a leader in the national dialogue to improve policies and practices enabling financial wellness, is working to ensure that global economic progress benefits all members of tomorrow's workforce.

Prudential is dedicated to developing the talent of the future, with a focus on people from traditionally underserved and underrepresented markets. This requires a portfolio of strategic partnerships, supported by a $180 million commitment through 2025 to provide young people with the training and tools to access the job market and get on a path to financial security. Opportunity Youth represent a large untapped talent pool. With an eye towards employer demand, and a strong return on student and employer outcomes, these commitments are allowing innovative models to improve, scale and sustain growth.

$1 Billion Milestone

Prudential has long recognized that its investments could—and should—combine social and financial return. This year, the company reached its goal of building a $1 billion impact investing portfolio by 2020.

These innovative models, which include pioneering organizations like General Assembly, Andela, YouthBuild and Per Scholas, help young adults develop the technical skills they need for the 21st century workforce. Graduates of these programs move from minimum-wage jobs to career-track positions, helping to build an inclusive workforce and ensure sustainable financial wellness for themselves, their families and their communities—and employers are provided with solutions to persistent talent shortages.

Since July 2017, Prudential has recruited 68 candidates from its portfolio of skills-training program partners for internships, contractor positions and full-time hires. Of these candidates, 96 percent were people of color; 62 percent were female. Complemented by ongoing efforts to recruit and retain diverse traditional talent, these non-traditional talent models are empowering and transforming the workforce of the future – both in and outside of Prudential.

Spotlight on Talent When financial constraints kept Shanelle Forde from finishing her college education, she worked a number of jobs simultaneously to make ends meet. "I also knew that I didn't want to continue like that," she said. Today, Shanelle is a graduate of the software development track at Year Up, a one-year intensive training program that provides skills training and career support to diverse, low-income young adults ages 18-24. After completing a six-month internship with Prudential's Chief Investment Office, Prudential hired Shanelle as a systems development associate.

185

Board Oversight of our People Strategy

The Board is actively engaged in oversight of human capital management. Annually, the Board meets to review our succession strategy and leadership pipeline for key roles, including the CEO, taking into account the Corporation's long-term corporate strategy. More broadly, the Board is regularly informed on key talent indicators for the overall workforce, including performance against diversity metrics with respect to representation, hiring, promotions, and leadership. Talent management and employee engagement metrics and goals are included in the strategic and operational performance measures in management's annual incentive program. The Board also reviews our annual employee engagement survey results. The Board is updated on the Corporation's People Strategy on an annual basis, which is refined based on business drivers, the changing internal and external environment, and the future of work. Board members also are active partners, engaging and spending time with our high potential leaders throughout the year at Board meetings and other events.

In 2019, Lockheed Martin transitioned from the term "Human Capital Management" to "People Strategy" which conveys our commitment to expanding our talent pipeline and critical skills to build our future workforce. Lockheed Martin's People Strategy is tightly aligned with our business needs and technology strategy. We continue to respond with agile solutions to internal and external environmental shifts, which includes delivering a robust pipeline of talent to support future business growth, remain competitive and to attract, develop, motivate and retain our workforce.

186

Enterprise Risk and Sustainability Priorities

To build integrated assurance, enterprise risk and sustainability are managed jointly in one department and mutually reinforced through the following processes:

- **Risk Identification:** We monitor a dynamic risk universe that includes ESG topics prevalent in voluntary frameworks, mandatory regulations, and internally identified sources.
- **Risk Assessment:** We prioritize and evaluate assumptions from a diverse set of risk topics that are relevant to strategic and operational objectives. This includes examining environmental and social factors applicable to risk topics in our business.
- **Risk Controls and Mitigation:** Through the Risk Audit Strategy Board (a periodic, rigorous examination of the intersection between our Enterprise Risk heat map index and our internal audit plan) we mitigate risk related to several ESG factors, and we track, measure and report our performance for greater transparency. This process also informs how we evaluate the effectiveness of controls for risk elements identified through our enterprise risk assessments, corporate policies and internal audits.

These linkages extend to operational elements of our business. Our **Employee Wellbeing** core issue emphasizes talent recruitment and talent development, two factors essential to identifying critical skills and helping employees reach their full potential. In alignment with our **Information Security** core issue, we educate and direct suppliers to resources to strengthen their abilities to counter data security and privacy threats, which are integral to our buying decisions. We teach small and disadvantaged businesses how to increase operational efficiency and manage ethics and sustainability impacts as stressed in our **Business Integrity** core issue.

187

| Our Company | Our Approach | Business Integrity | Product Impact | Employee Wellbeing | Resource Efficiency | Information Security | Appendix | 2019 Sustainability Report | Lockheed Martin | 31

Employee Wellbeing Overview | Workplace safety and wellness | Talent development | Talent recruitment | Diversity and inclusion

Employee Wellbeing Overview

OBJECTIVE
Creating a high-performance, inclusive workplace culture that engages employees and creates rewarding career paths for our current and future workforce.

Importance
A key to Lockheed Martin's success is enabling employees to apply their passion for purposeful innovation. This helps us attract and retain diverse talent who want to do meaningful work and enhances our competitiveness as a next-generation technology company and employer of choice. We prioritize talent recruitment, talent development, workplace safety, and diversity and inclusion to address the changing workforce, meet customer needs, and innovate for the future.

Challenge
Because employees are our greatest asset, we are committed to investing in all aspects of the employee experience. We recruit talent based on skill, diversity, and program needs. The new world of work accelerates the demand for digital-based skills, and as the necessary skill sets shift with the advent of new technologies, we adjust our priorities. This includes adapting our human resources focus to make sure we remain well-positioned to continue meeting our customers' ever-changing needs. Our challenge is to provide business intelligence tools, skills development, and targeted recruitment strategies to keep our business and our employees ahead of evolving workforce trends.

TIER 1

Workplace Safety and Wellness

Talent Development

Talent Recruitment

Diversity and Inclusion

TIER 2

STEM Education

DID YOU KNOW?

Lockheed Martin is partnering with Catalyst, a global nonprofit organization dedicated to building more inclusive workplaces, and has committed $2.5 million in support of its campaign, "Now is the Moment – Be a Catalyst".

THE
SCIENCE

Future space travel, autonomous machines, and national defense arsenals rely on the scientists and technologists we hire to push the boundaries of their fields. We motivate employees through our talent development, inclusion, wellbeing and benefits programs and our mission to innovate a better future.

OF
CITIZENSHIP

Talented, resilient, and engaged employees drive performance and innovation. Our employees generate wide-ranging societal solutions to complex global challenges.

188

| Our Company | Our Approach | Business Integrity | Product Impact | Employee Wellbeing | Resource Efficiency | Information Security | Appendix | 2019 Sustainability Report | Lockheed Martin   36

Employee Wellbeing Overview   Workplace Safety and Wellness   Talent Development   Talent Recruitment   Diversity and Inclusion

Diversity and Inclusion

OBJECTIVE
Creating a workplace that fosters a sense of belonging and where the diverse talents and unique perspectives of our people drive affordable and innovative solutions for our customers and business success.

Management
Diversity and inclusion are the foundation of our culture and reflect our values of doing what's right, respecting others, and performing with excellence. Our initiatives center on creating a workplace where employees feel welcome, respected, engaged, and encouraged to thrive. We implement strategies and initiatives that promote inclusive behaviors and equip leaders and employees with resources and toolkits that allow them to better understand and embrace the value of diversity and inclusion. Such toolkits focus on effective engagement strategies and provide information and key insights on topics that empower all employees. Additionally, we provide opportunities for our Business Resource Groups (BRGs) to make a sustainable impact on our business, culture, and people by bringing increased visibility to the key role communities and BRGs play within our organization.

Goals
☑ Develop the best workforce for our customers by increasing representation of women, people of color, veterans, and people with disabilities.

Progress
This year, we increased our representation of People of Color by 1.5%. Our representation of people with disabilities, veterans, and women remained flat as compared to 2018 workforce demographics.

☑ Increase employee participation in company-sponsored diversity events, Business Resource Groups (BRGs), and leadership associations.

Progress
The number of BRG events increased by 4.9% and participation increased by 35.5% as compared to 2018. We saw an overall increase of 9% in Leadership Forum.

WOMEN AT LOCKHEED MARTIN
Lockheed Martin is proud to have a team of incredible women dedicated to designing and building technology and tools that support our customers across the globe. These women are paving the way and inspiring the next generation of girls and young women who will one day work in STEM fields.

We launched the Women in the Workplace initiative to increase the representation of women across the company, ensuring that hiring and promotions are fair and offering leaders as many opportunities to engage, champion, and lead diversity-related dialogues and events that help develop all leaders as champions of diversity and inclusion.

Engagement with Society of Women Engineers (SWE)
44 SWE offers were accepted
39.0% increase from 2018
Engagements include:
- National Outreach
- STEM K-12 Females
- SWENext Outreach
- Scholarships

28 women graduated from the Program Management Talent Institute in 2019
10.0% increase in the number of women who received a promotion since they began their Program Management Talent Institute experience between 2018 and 2019

21,273 members participated in the Women's Impact Network
70.7% of all leaders have participated in an Effective Leadership of Inclusive Teams experience

Ranked #2 Top Employer – Women Engineer Magazine

Representation of women in all levels of leadership increased year-over-year from 2018.

Sponsorships and volunteering to support girls and women in STEM programs:
- Girls Inc.
- Imagine Science
- STEM Conference for Girls
- Project Lead the Way
- 4H
42.0% of the 200 STEM Scholarship Program recipients are female

189

Examples of Turnover Cost Calculations

Step by Step Calculation of Turnover Costs

Susan - Info Sys Architect

Step 1 — Calculating Benchmark Employee Costs

Departing Employee Annual Base Salary	$150,000.00	<---Enter Salary here
Calculated Annual Benefits	$30,000.00	Estimated 20% of base salary
Calculated Monthly Salary +Benefits	$15,000.00	
Calculated Daily Salary + Benefits	$782.61	Based on 230 eight hour workdays

Step 2 — Cost of Covering the Vacant Position
*****Calculated as Other Employees Filling in While Vacant

Number of days until position is filled	60	<---Enter Days here
Calculated Daily Cost of covering vacancy	$258.26	33% of Departed Employees Daily Salary + Benefits
Calculated Total Cost to Cover the Position	$15,495.65	

Step 3 — Cost to Fill a Vacant Position

HR / Hiring Managers Annual Salary	$175,000.00	<---Enter Salary here
Calculated HR / Hiring Managers Hourly Rate	$114.13	Based on 230 eight hour workdays and 20% fringe rate
Cost of Advertising (Online/Print/Recruiter)	$30,000.00	<---Enter dollar value here
Cost of Resume Screening	10	<---Enter Number of HOURS
Cost of Interviews (phone, 1st, 2nd, etc)	20	<---Enter Number of HOURS
Cost of Backgroung Checks	$500.00	<---Enter dollar value here
Calculated Total Cost to Fill Vacant Position	$33,923.91	

Step 4 — Onboarding and Orientation Costs

Trainer / Hiring Manager Annual Salary	$175,000.00	<---Enter Salary here
Calculated Trainer / Hiring Manager Daily Rate	$913.04	Based on 230 eight hour workdays and 20% fringe rate
Total Training Days	10	<---Enter number of days
Calculated Total Onboarding Orientation Costs	$9,130.43	

Step 5 — Cost of Productivity Ramp Up
*During first 3 months, an average new employee performs 50% productivity of a tenured top performer

Calculated Daily employee Costs (salary & benefits)	$782.61	Assumes same rate as departed employee from Step 1
Number of Working days in First 3 months	58	<---Enter Days (avg 58)
Calcuated Cost of Productivity Ramp Up	$22,695.65	

RESULTS — FINAL TURNOVER COST CALCULATION

Calculated Total Turnover Cost for Departed Employee	$81,245.65	
Number of Employees Lost in the Last 12 Months	1	<---Enter number of employees lost
Estimated Annual Cost of Turnover	$81,245.65	

190

Scenario Background: At the time of this case, the plant was averaging an annual, historic backorder level of 60% on 1 billion doses (all different products, at different COGS, CPU, and margins).
Annual average labor cost increase, at the time of this transaction, were 3-5% per year for the 2 years prior. Average annual labor costs are pressured to be higher, as the labor market has tightened significantly and the facility is in a real area with < 3.4% unemployment rate

	Annual Plant Cost Increase %	Future Unit Volume Increase %	Total Employees		Total Plant units of production	Average Cost per unit	Total $ Production Cost/Value	Total $ Production per Employee	Sales Value per unit MFG MFG cost	Total $ Sales Value	Total $ Sales per Employee
	2%	3.0%	299		1,000,000,000	$0.20	$200,000,000	666,500	$ 2.00	$2,000,000,000	6,680,000

	Annual per Person			Annual "Machine" Total/Average					
	# Machine Operators	Total Labor Cost	Total # of Operators	Units produced per Machine	Average Cost per unit	Total $ production per Machine	Total Units produced by all machines	Total $ production all Machines	Average $ Production value per Machine	$ Production value per Operator
	5	$60,360	12	20,000,000	$0.20	$4,000,000	240,000,000	$48,000,000	$4,000,000	$4,000,000

	Positions Eliminated	Labor Cost $ Impact	% MFG Change	# Machines Impacted	MFG Unit Change	Average Cost per unit	Lost Production $ Impact	$ Sales Lost Revenue	Backorder Impact (Units)	Prodtion Savings Impact	Base Year NET ROI $ Impact	Total 5 Year Impact
Low Impact Scenario $ Impact of a change in MFG capacity in 1 Machine	1	$60,360	-10%	1	(2,000,000)	$0.20	-$400,000	-$4,000,000	2,200,000	$60,360	-$3,940,000	-$21,770,967
High Impact Scenario #2. $ Impact of a % change in MFG capacity in 12 Machines	1	$60,360	-10%	12	(24,000,000)	$0.20	-$4,800,000	-$48,000,000	24,000,000	$60,360	-$47,940,000	-$264,898,762

* = rounded to nearest $000

191

Index

(IFAC) 5, 54, 63, 92, 103, 258, 259, 262, 263

International Financial Reporting Standards (IFRS) 22, 32, 33, 35, 38, 51, 55, 58, 103, 256, 258

International Integrated Reporting Coalition (IIRC) 5, 20, 22, 23, 26, 59, 62, 67, 92, 255, 256, 259

International Labour Organization (ILO) 200, 203, 265

International Standards Organization, see also ISO 30414 and ISO 30415 67, 68, 69, 196, 197, 198, 199, 201, 203, 205, 206, 207, 208, 209, 210, 212, 214, 215, 216, 217, 219, 220, 222, 225, 226, 227, 228, 229, 260, 264, 265, 266, 267, 268, 269

Investor(s) 1, 2, 22, 23, 26, 28, 34, 35, 37, 38, 39, 40, 41, 42, 43, 44, 46, 47, 48, 49, 50, 54, 55, 56, 58, 59, 62, 64, 65, 67, 74, 76, 83, 88, 91, 94, 95, 96, 97, 98, 99, 106, 109, 110, 111, 121, 122, 124, 125, 126, 135, 144, 145, 157, 256, 257, 259, 260, 262, 263

Irrational Capital, see also Ariely, Dan 78, 85

IRS 10-K 94, 96

ISO 30414

    ISO 30414

        4.7.3 - Costs (3) 201

        4.7.12 (4) 214

    ISO 30414 4.7.2 (1) 203

    ISO 30414 4.7.3 (1&2) 228, 229

    ISO 30414 4.7.5(3) 216

    ISO 30414 4.7.7 209, 212

    ISO 30414 4.7.8 (1) 227, 229

ISO 30414 4.7.8 (2) 227, 229

ISO 30414 4.7.9 (5, 6, 9) 219, 220

ISO 30414 4.7.9 (11) 222, 225

ISO 30414 4.7.10 (1) 217, 220

ISO 30414 4.7.10 (2) 216

ISO 30414, see also International Standards Organization and ISO 30415 68, 69, 196, 197, 198, 201, 203, 205, 207, 208, 209, 212, 214, 215, 216, 217, 219, 220, 222, 225, 227, 228, 229, 260, 264, 265, 266, 267, 268, 269

ISO 30415

    ISO 30415

        8.6.2.3 198

        8.6.3.1, 8.6.3.2 199

    ISO 30415, see also International Standards Organization and ISO 30414 69, 198, 199, 206, 207, 208, 260, 265

J

Job Creation 221

Juniper Agency (or Juniper Productions) 5, 189, 264

JUST Capital 22, 28, 61, 256

Just Cause, see also Sinek, Simon 75, 127, 144

K

Kendi, Ibram X. 111, 112, 264

Key Performance Indicator (KPI) 61, 67, 107, 170, 226

246 | LAURA KELLERS QUEEN

Kim, Sarah 5, 96, 97, 99, 263

Kirkpatrick, Donald 67, 219, 220, 267

KPMG 53

Kramer, Mark 95, 263

Kuhn, Thomas, see also Paradigm 87, 262

L

Language 2, 13, 18, 19, 25, 28, 58, 69, 70, 74, 79, 87, 95, 105, 110, 155, 156, 162, 163

Lawler, Edward 107

Leader(s) 1, 5, 11, 15, 16, 18, 20, 24, 33, 37, 54, 64, 75, 81, 87, 89, 90, 91, 92, 97, 105, 109, 111, 116, 117, 129, 137, 138, 141, 147, 151, 152, 154, 156, 161, 169, 172, 173, 188, 216, 255, 262

Leadership 1, 20, 22, 31, 53, 68, 76, 80, 81, 90, 99, 102, 115, 116, 117, 126, 127, 137, 138, 148, 151, 173, 174, 180, 183, 198, 216, 217, 261

Leadership development 216

Learning and development 216

LGBTQ+ 88, 109, 148

Limited Partner (LP), see also Investor(s) 40, 49, 96, 97, 98, 110

Listening 84, 85, 102, 128, 134, 137, 139, 141, 147, 162

Living Wage 204, 205, 208, 266

Living wage (percent) 204, 208

Lockheed Martin 50

Logan, Denise 5

London School of Business 45

Loper, J. Renay 5, 144

Lost Time 209

M

Manufactured Capital, see also Capital(s) 26

Martin, Roger 101, 263

Mastagni, Aeisha 5, 96

Materiality 16, 25, 41, 42, 47, 48, 49, 54, 55, 56, 57, 59, 70, 73, 83, 105, 109, 144, 164, 227, 258, 260

Mayo, Anthony 88

McGannon, Brian 84

McKinsey & Company 45, 90, 110, 257, 262, 264

Measures 1, 19, 26, 41, 53, 56, 57, 59, 68, 73, 79, 83, 92, 100, 107, 109, 143, 171, 173, 198, 200, 201, 204, 205, 208, 216, 217, 218, 219, 220, 221, 222, 226, 227, 229

Mergers and Acquisitions, see also Transactions 1, 9, 12, 83, 118, 121, 156, 158, 160, 169, 172, 173, 182, 183, 184, 185, 189, 261

Metrics 1, 27, 41, 47, 53, 54, 56, 59, 63, 66, 67, 68, 69, 70, 71, 77, 79, 93, 94, 96, 98, 99, 107, 143, 170, 171, 195, 196, 197, 199, 200, 201, 203, 204, 205, 207, 209, 210, 212, 214, 215, 216, 217, 218, 220, 221, 222, 223, 225, 226, 227, 228, 229, 255, 256, 257, 258, 259, 260, 261, 266, 267, 268

MIT Living Wage Calculator 204, 205, 266

Mohindra, Amit 5, 87, 262

Montemari, Marco 34

More Deeds 111, 112, 142, 143

Morgan Stanley 46, 257

Most Valuable Asset(s) 116, 120

Muddy Boots 137, 141

Multi-Stakeholder, see also Stakeholder(s)
25, 61, 62, 82, 94, 110, 111, 153

N

NASDAQ 88, 127, 145, 262

Natural Language Processing (NLP) 79, 82

Newkirk, Pamela 147, 154

NewROI Experience 189

Nolan, Robert 5

Non-governmental organizations (NGOs)
21, 22

Nonprofit(s) 28, 54, 58, 109, 128, 138, 139,
140, 141, 147

Nordstrom 82

O

Occupational Accidents 209

Occupational Safety and Health Administration, see also OSHA 16, 22, 69, 209,
210, 214, 215, 266

OECD

Getting Skills Right

Future Ready Adult Learning
Systems 219

Okuji-Wilson, Kelli 5

Organisation for Economic Cooperation
and Development (OECD) 23, 57, 215,
219, 220, 267

OSHA 29 CFR 1904 210

Outward Mindset 102, 103, 263

P

Palokoff, Kathy 5

Papillon, Kimberly 155

Paradigm 18, 87, 90, 92, 104, 105, 111, 262

Pay 27, 28, 32, 35, 39, 60, 83, 85, 109, 127,
133, 134, 138, 152, 174, 195, 198, 201,
206, 207, 215, 227, 256

Pay Equality Percent 195, 198

Pay Equity 28

Pay Gap (percent and ratio) 195, 201,
207

Ratio of average salary and remuneration 201

Ratio of basic salary and remuneration
of women to men 198

Ratio of CEO compensation to employees 199

Ratios of standard entry level wage by
gender compared to local minimum
wage 199, 206

People Alpha, see also Alpha 18, 41, 47, 65,
124, 255

People Economics 1, 2, 18, 19, 25, 31, 45,
73, 88

People of Color 17, 109

People Pillar, see also Four Pillar Approach
and World Economic Forum (WEF) 68,
69, 205, 207, 214, 220

People, see also Worker(s) and Employees
1, 2, 5, 9, 10, 12, 13, 14, 16, 17, 18, 19, 20,

Trust, see also Cultures and Engagement 48, 58, 73, 97, 261

Turnover 68, 83, 106, 107, 119, 120, 174, 181, 184, 221, 222, 225, 237

Turnover rate 222, 225

U

United Nations Sustainability and Development Goals (SDGs) 24, 29, 31, 32, 42, 57, 69, 200, 220

United Stated Forum for Sustainable and Responsible Investment (US SIF) 84

United States Congress 22

United States Department of Labor (DoL) 23, 43, 266

United States Securities and Exchange Commission (SEC) 23, 48, 49, 54, 55, 59, 65, 68, 88, 96, 121, 123, 124, 206

U.S.C. §§ 151-169 204, 207

V

Valuation 1, 14, 18, 65, 66, 67, 97, 98, 115, 118, 121, 122, 123, 124, 125

Value (Business, Company or Organizational) 33, 49, 64, 92, 97, 103, 121, 181, 220, 226

Value Leakage 93, 98

Value Reporting Foundation, see also International Integrated Reporting Council (IIRC) and Sustainability Accounting Standards Board (SASB) 22, 23

Values, see also Culture 2, 36, 49, 66, 74, 80, 83, 87, 101, 108, 110, 127, 129, 137, 141, 165, 172, 182, 227

Venture Capital (VC) 39, 40

W

Wage Level Percent 195, 198, 206

Washington, Paul 50, 94

WBCSD Measuring Impact Framework 218, 220

Weber, Lauren 154

Webster, Lee 68

WEF/IBC Measuring Stakeholder Capitalism

Skills for the future 218

Weighted Average Cost of Capital (WACC) 122

Welch, Jack 158

Well-being 25, 29, 36, 60, 63, 68, 71, 73, 81, 109, 135, 208, 209, 212, 215

Willis Towers Watson 73, 93, 94, 261, 262

Wolfe, David 75, 261

Work Environments, see also Cultures 5, 16, 18, 71, 73, 76, 138, 174, 209, 211, 213, 217, 262, 266

Workers

Workers covered by an occupational health and safety management system 210

Workers covered by an occupational health and safety management system 210

Workers, see also Employees 1, 9, 11, 12, 15, 16, 17, 27, 28, 46, 47, 49, 50, 58, 71, 92, 101, 104, 108, 109, 117, 129, 165, 198, 199, 204, 209, 210, 211, 212, 213, 214, 228, 264

Z

Endnotes

1   David Brooks, *The Road to Character* (New York: Penguin Random House, 2015).

2   Larry Fink, "Letter to CEOs" (2018), https://www.blackrock.com/corporate/investor-relations/2018-larry-fink-ceo-letter.

3   Dave Bookbinder, *The NEW ROI: Return on Individuals* (Mount Laurel, NJ: Limelight Publishing, 2017).

iii

4   Adam Smith, *The Wealth of Nations* (New York, NY: Bantam Dell, 2003).

5   Milton Friedman, "The Social Responsibility of Business is to Increase its Profits," *New York Times Magazine* (September 30, 1970).

6   Frederick Winslow Taylor. *The Principles of Scientific Management* (New York, NY and London: Harper & Brothers, 1911).

7   Upton Sinclair, *The Jungle* (Dover Publications, 2001).

8   Klaus Schwab, "Davos Manifesto 1973: A Code of Ethics for Business Leaders." https://www.weforum.org/agenda/2019/12/davos-manifesto-1973-a-code-of-ethics-for-business-leaders/

9   Adam Smith, *Theory of Moral Sentiments* (San Francisco, CA: Stephen Buck, 2017)

10   Laura Kellers Queen, "People Alpha: Identifying Where the Workforce Fits into PE's Return Equation" (2020). https://alphacalc.com/wp-content/uploads/2020/04/29-Bison-People-Alpha-3.20-3.pdf.

11   Capitals Coalition, "Principles of Integrated Capitals Assessments" (January 2021). https"//capitalscoalition.org/wp-content/cuploads/2021/01/Pinciples_of_integrated_capitals_assessments_final.pdf.

12   "IIRC and SASB announce intent to merge in major step towards simplifying the corporate reporting system" (November 25, 2020). https://integratedreporting.org/news/iirc-and-sasb-announce-intent-to-merge-in-major-step-towards-simplifying-the -corporate-reporting-system/.

13   Diligent. "Measuring Stakeholder Capitalism: ESG, Metrics & The Board's Role" (June 16, 2020).

14   IIRC, "International <IR> Framework" (January 2021). https://integratedreporting.org/wp-content/uploads/2021/01/InternationalIntegratedReportingFramework.pdf.

15   World Economic Forum, "Toward Common Metrics and Consistent Reporting of Sustainable Value Creation," (January 2020). https://www.weforum.org/whitepapers/toward-common-metrics-and-consistent-reporting-of-sustainable-value-creation.

16   Government Equalities Office. "Gender pay gap reporting: Overview." (December 14, 2020). https://www.gov.uk/guidance/gender-pay-gap-reporting-overview.

17   GRI 102: General Disclosures 2016.

18   JUST Capital, "JUST Rankings 2021 on how the largest U.S. corporations perform on the "issues that matter most to the American public" for 2020. https://justcapital.com/reports/announcing-the-2021-rankings-of-americas-most-just-companies/.

19   United Nations, "The 17 Goals." https://sdgs.un.org/goals.

20   IFRS Foundation, "IAS 38 Intangible Assets." https://www.ifrs.org/issued-standars-/list-of-standards/ias-38-intangible-assets/.

21   M. Montemari, M.S. Chiucci, M. Gatti. (2019) "Every Cloud Has a Silver Lining: A History of Barriers to Intellectual Capital Measurement," *International Journal of Business and Management*, Vol. 14, No. 11, 139–152.

22   D. Andriessen (2001). "Weightless Wealth: Four modifications to standard IC theory." *Journal of Intellectual Capital*, Vol. 2, No. 3, 204–214.

23   Leif Edvinsson and Michael Malone. *Intellectual Capital: Realizing Your Company's True Value by Finding Its Hidden Brain Power* (New York, NY: Harper-Collins Publishers, 1997).

24   International Financial Reporting Standards Foundation. "Spotlight – Intangible resources and financial reporting – an evolving debate." (July 2019). https://www.ifrs.org/investor-ventre/investor-update-hub/july-2019/.

25   IIRC, "International <IR> Framework" (January 2021). https://integratedreporting.org/wp-content/uploads/2021/01/InternationalIntegratedReportingFramework.pdf.

26   J. Dumay (2012). "Grand theories as barriers to using IC concepts." *Journal of Intellectual Capital*, Vol. 13, No. 1, 4–15.

27   Jon Hale. "Sustainable Funds U.S. Landscape Report: Record flows and strong performance in 2019. (February 14, 2020). *Morningstar.*

28   Jon Hale. "Sustainable Funds U.S. Landscape Report: Record flows and strong performance in 2019. (February 14, 2020). *Morningstar.*

29   Jon Hale. "Sustainable Funds U.S. Landscape Report: Record flows and strong performance in 2019. *Morningstar* (February 14, 2020).

30   Eugene Scalia. "Retiree's Security Trumps Other Social Goals: A new Labor Department rule reinforces pension funds' fiduciary duties." *Wall Street Journal* (June 23, 2020).

31   Alex Edmans. "The link between job satisfaction and firm value, with implications for corporate social responsibility." *Academy of Management Perspectives*, Vol. 26, No.4, 1–19 (November 2012).

32   Hortense de la Bouteriere, Alberto Montagner, Angelika Reich. "Unlocking success in digital transformations" (October 29, 2018). McKinsey & Company. https://www.mckinsey.com/business-functions/organization/our-insights/unlocking-success-in-digital-transformations.

33   "Rise of the SHEconomy" Morgan Stanley (September 23, 2019). https://www.morganstanley.com/ideas/womens-impact-on-the-economy.

34   Nicole Bateman and Martha Ross. "Why has COVID-19 been especially harmful for working women?" The Brookings Institute (Washington, DC. October 2020). https://www.brookings.edu/essay/why-has-covid-19-been-especially-harmful-for-working-women/.

35   Apax.com/media/2485/apax-sustainability-report_edition-8.pdf,

36   Bank of America, "2020 Human Capital Management Report," http://investor.bankofamerica.com/news-releases/news-release-details/bank-america-issues-2020-human -capital-management-report,

37   Diligent. "Measuring Stakeholder Capitalism: ESG, Metrics & The Board's Role" (June 16, 2020). https://www.youtube.com/watch?v=Z01FXfeSESo.

38   Larry Fink. "Letter to CEOs" (2019). Blackrock.com/Americas-offshore/en/2019-larry-fink-ceo-letter.

39   Human Capital Management Coalition (HCMC), "Petition for Rulemaking." (July 6, 2017). sec.gov/rules/petitions/2017/petn4-711.pdf.

40   Jay Clayton. "Modernizing the Framework for Business, Legal Proceedings and Risk Factor Disclosures" (August 26, 2020). Sec.gov/public-statement/clayton-regulation-s-k-2020-08-26.

41   Rep. Cynthia Axne. "H.R.5930 – Workforce Investment Disclosure Act." Congress.gov/bill/116th-congress/house-bill/5930.

42   Human Capital Management Coalition. uawtrust.org/hcmc.

43   The Conference Board (2020). Human Capital: A New Era in Disclosure. https://conference-board.org/webcasts/ondemand/human-capital-management

44   Peter Cappelli. "Stop Overengineering People Management" *Harvard Business Review* (September–October 2020).

45   International Accounting Standard-38 (IAS 38) "Intangible Assets." https://www.ifrs.org/issued-standards/list-of-standards/ias-38-intangible-assets.

46   Statista. "Value of the tangible and intangible assets of the five biggest companies on the S&P 500 worldwide from 1975 to 2018" (February 2020). https://www.statista.com/statistics/1113984/intangible-tangible-assets-sandp500-largest-companies/.

47   Ocean Tomo. "Intangible Asset Market Value Study" (Calendar Year 2020). oceantomo.com.

48   World Economic Forum-International Business Coalition. "Measuring Stakeholder Capitalism: Toward Common Metrics and Consistent Reporting of Sustainable Value Creation" (September 22, 2020). weforum.org/reports/measuring-stakeholder-capitalism-towards-common-metrics-and-consistent-reporting-og-sustainable-value-creation/

49   IFAC. "IFAC Supports World Economic Forum Initiative. Consultation Draft: Toward Common Metrics and Consistent Reporting of Sustainable Value Creation." https://www.ifac.org/system/files/publications/files/IFAC-World-Economic-Forum-Consultation-Response-ESG-Value-Creation.pdf.

50   International Financial Reporting Standards Foundation. "IFRS Practice Statement 2: Making Materiality Judgements" (September 2017). https://www.ifrs.org/-/mediaproject/disclosure-initiative/disclosure-initiative-materiality-practice-statement/mps-project-summary-and-oractice-statement.pdf.

51   https://www.sasb.org/standards-overview/.

52   United Nations Principles for Responsible Investment. "What are the Principles for Responsible Investment?." https://www.unpri.org/pri/

what-are-the-principles-for-responsible-investment.

53   https://www.ceres.org/.

54   Global Reporting Initiative. "Welcome to GRI." https://www.globalreporting.org. GRI content is used with permission. Global Reporting Initiative (GRI) is the independent international organization – headquartered in Amsterdam with regional offices around the world – that help businesses, governments and other organizations understand and communicate their sustainability impacts.

55   Human Capital Management Coalition (HCMC). http://uawtrust.org/hcmc.

56   Human Capital Management Coalition. "July 2017 Press Release." http:uawtrust.org/AdminCenter/Library.Files/Media/501/Press%20Releases/2017/17julyhcmcpressrelease.pdf.

57   Facilitated by the Impact Management Project, World Economic Forum and Deloitte the *Statement of Intent to Work Together Towards Comprehensive Corporate Reporting* (September 2020) is a joint initiative of the CDP, CDSB, GRI, IIRC and SASB. https://29kjwb3armds2g3gi4lq2sx1-wpengine.netdna-ssl.com/wp-content/uploads/Statement-of-Intent-to-Work-Together-Towards-Comprehensive-Corporate-Reporting.pdf

58   World Economic Forum. "Toward Common Metrics and Consistent Reporting of Sustainable Value Creation." (September 2020). https://www.weforum.org/whitepapers/toward-common-metrics-and-consistent-reporting-of-sustainable-value-creation. All WEF content is provided under licensure and used with permission.

59   IIRC, "International <IR> Framework" (January 2021). https://integratedreporting.org/wp-content/uploads/2021/01/InternationalIntegratedReportingFramework.pdf.

60   International Federation of Accountants (IFAC). "Understanding Value Creation." (2020) https://www.ifac.org/system/files/publications/files/Understanding-Value-Creation_0.pdf.

61   World Economic Forum. "Davos Manifesto 2020: The Universal Purpose of a Company in the Fourth Industrial Revolution" (December 2019). https://weforum.org/agenda/2019/12/davos-manifesto-2020-the-universal-purpose-of-a-company-in-the-fourth-industrial-revolution/.

62   Jay Clayton. "Clayton Remarks Investor Advisory Committee Call" (February 6, 2019). https://www.sec.gov/public-statement/clayton-remarks-investor-advisory-committee-call-020619.

63   Tideline and Impact Capital Managers. "The Alpha in Impact: How operating with an impact objective can add financial value for investors" (December 2018). https://tideline.com/wp-content/uploads/2020/11/Tideline-ICM-Alpha_in_Impact.pdf.

64   N. G. Flamholtz. "Toward a theory of human resource value in formal organizations." *The Accounting Review*, Vol. 47, No.4, 66–78 (1972).

65   J. Fitz-enz. "The measurement Imperative." *Personnel Journal*, Vol. 54, No. 9 (1978).

66   M. Rahaman, A. Hossain, T. Akter. "Problem with Human Resource Accounting and a Possible Solution" *Research Journal of Finance and Accounting*. Vol.4, No. 18, 1–10 (2013).

67   Jahahar Lal in M. Rahaman, A. Hossain, T. Akter. "Problem with Human Resource Accounting and a Possible Solution." *Research Journal of Finance and Accounting*. Vol.4, No. 18, 1–10 (2013).

68   S.M. Sheffrin. *Economics: Principle in Action*. (Upper Saddle River, NJ: Pearson Prentice Hall. 2003).

69   International Standards Organization. *Human resource management – Guidelines for internal and external human capital reporting* (ISO 30414:2018(E)). All International Standards Organization (ISO) content is used with permission, American National Standards Institute (ANSI).

70   International Standards Organization. *Human resource management – Diversity and Inclusion* (ISO 30415:2021(E)).

71   Lee S. Webster. "Materiality of Human Capital Metrics." (April 29, 2019). https://www.sec.gov/comments/4-711/4711-5453156-184911.pdf.

72   World Economic Forum. "Toward Common Metrics and Consistent Reporting of Sustainable Value Creation." (September 2020). https://www.weforum.org/whitepapers/toward-common-metrics-and-consistent-reporting-of-sustainable-value-creation.

73   World Economic Forum. "Toward Common Metrics and Consistent Reporting of Sustainable Value Creation." (September 2020). https://www.weforum.org/whitepapers/toward-common-metrics-and-consistent-reporting-of-sustainable-value-creation.

74   World Economic Forum. "Toward Common Metrics and Consistent Reporting of Sustainable Value Creation." (September 2020). https://www.weforum.org/whitepapers/toward-common-metrics-and-consistent-reporting-of-sustainable-value-creation.

75   World Economic Forum. "Toward Common Metrics and Consistent Reporting of Sustainable Value Creation." (September 2020). https://www. weforum.org/whitepapers/toward-common-metrics-and-consistent-reporting-of-sustainable-value-creation.

76   Paul J. Zack. "The Neuroscience of Trust," *Harvard Business Review* (January–February 2017).

77   Willis Towers Watson. "The Power of Three: Taking Engagement to New Heights" (May 7, 2019). https://willistowerswatson.com/en-US/insights/2016/02/The-Power-of-Three--Taking-Engagement-to-New-Heights.

78   Coalition for Inclusive Capitalism. "Embankment Project for Inclusive Capitalism Report." (2020). https://www.coalitionforinclusivecapitalism.com/wp-contet/uploads/2021/01/coalition-epic-report.pdf.

79   Edgar H. Schein. *Organizational Culture and Leadership*. (San Francisco, CA: Jossey-Bass, 1985).

80   Simon Sinek. *The Infinite Game*. (Penguin Random House LLC, 2019).

81   R. Sisodia, J. Sheth, D. Wolfe. *Firms of Endearment: How World-Class Companies Profit from Passion and Purpose*. (Upper Saddle River, NJ: Pearson Education. 2014).

82   Dan Ariely and Doug Claffey. "Align your culture efforts to drive performance." (October 2020). https://www.energage.com/align-your-culture-efforts- to-drive-performance/. Note: Energage is a registered trademark of Energage, LLC used with permission.

83   Dan Ariely and Doug Claffey. "Align your culture efforts to drive performance." (October 2020). https://www.energage.com/align-your-culture-efforts-to-drive-performance/.

84   Dan Ariely and Doug Claffey. "Align your culture efforts to drive performance." (October 2020). https://www.energage.com/align-your-culture-efforts-to-drive-performance/.

85   Coalition for Inclusive Capitalism. "Embankment Project for Inclusive Capitalism Report." (2020).

86   Laura Kellers Queen. (2014) "Executives' attributes in high-stakes decision-making: A case study." https://search.proquest.com/openview/e437d-c23a5de04f431a991e29ecc689c/1?pq-origsite=gscholar&cbl=18750&diss=y.

87   Jeff Black. (2021) "People Risks in M&A – M&A Readiness Research" (Mercer). mercer.com/cpmtent/dam/mercer/private/gl-mergers-and-acquisi-

tions-people-risks-report-mercer.pdf.

88   Danny Nelms. (2020) " 2020 Retention Report." (Work Institute). info.
workinstitute.com/hubfs/2020%20Retention%20Report/Work%20Institutes%20
2020%20Retention%20Report.pdf

89   Dan Ariely and Doug Claffey. "Align your culture efforts to drive
performance." (October 2020). https://www.energage.com/align-your-culture-ef-
forts-to-drive-performance/

90   Thomas Kuhn. *The Structure of Scientific Revolutions* (3rd Edition).
Chicago, IL: University of Chicago Press, 1996).

91   Amit Mohindra. (2021) Personal interview conducted with the author
on January 11, 2021 via video conference.

92   NASDAQ. "Nasdaq to advance diversity through new proposed listing
requirements" (December 1, 2020) https://www.nasdaq.com/press-release/
nasdaq-to-advance-diversity-through-new-proposed-listing-require-
ments-2020-12-01.

93   Laura Morgan Roberts and Anthony J. Mayo. "Toward a racially just
workplace." *Harvard Business Review* (November 14, 2019).

94   Business Roundtable. "Statement on the Purpose of a Corporation."
opportunity.businessroundtable.org/ourcommitment.

95   McKinsey. "Reimagining the postpandemic organization." *McKinsey
Quarterly* (May 15, 2020).

96   IBM Institute for Business Value (2021). "Find your essential: How to
thrive in a post-pandemic reality. *C-Suite Series: The 2021 CEO Study*.

97   Larry Fink. (2020) "Letter to CEOs: A fundamental reshaping of
finance." https://blackrock.com/corporate/investor-relations/2020-lar-
ry-fink-ceo-letter.

98   International Federation of Accountants. "A Vision for the CFO &
Finance Function: From accounting for the balance sheet to accounting for the
business & value creation" (2019). ISBN: 978-1-60815-419-7. ifac.org/system/
files/publications/files/IFAC-Future-Fit-Accountant-V6-Singles.pdf.

99   HR People + Strategy and Willis Towers Watson. (January 2020) "The
Future Chief People Officer: Imagine. Invent. Ignite. Why empowered HR leaders
are key to capturing growth in the new world of work." Willistowerswatson.com/
en-US/Insights/2020/01/the-future-chief-people-officer-imagine-invent-ignite.

100   IBM Institute for Business Value. "Find your essential: How to thrive in a post-pandemic reality. *C-Suite Series: The 2021 CEO Study.*

101   R. Charan, D. Barton and D. Carey. :People Before Strategy: A New Role for the CHRO." (July- August 2015) *Harvard Business Review* (2021).

102   The Conference Board (2020). Human Capital: A New Era in Disclosure. https://conference-board.org/webcasts/ondemand/human-capital-management.

103   IBM Institute for Business Value (2021). "Find your essential: How to thrive in a post-pandemic reality. *C-Suite Series: The 2021 CEO Study.*

104   Michael E. Porter, George Serafeim, and Mark Kramer. "Where ESG Fails." (October 16, 2019) *Institutional Investor.* https://www.institutionalinvestors.com/article/b1hm5ghqtxj9s7/Where-ESG-Fails.

105   California State Teachers' Retirement System (CalSTRS). "CalSTRS Investment Beliefs." Calstrs.com/sites/main/files/file-attachments/calstrs_investment_beliefs.pdf.

106   The Conference Board (2020). Human Capital: A New Era in Disclosure. https://conference-board.org/webcasts/ondemand/human-capital-management.

107   Judy Samuelson. *The Six New Rules of Business: Creating Real Value in a Changing World.* (Oakland, CA: Berrett – Koehler Publishers, Inc. 2021).

108   Personal correspondence from Sarah Kim, formerly of Halyard Capital to the author (received February 20, 2021).

109   Coalition for Inclusive Capitalism. A Framework for Inclusive Capitalism (February 3, 2021). https://www.coalitionforinclusivecapitalism.com/event/a-framework-for-inclusive-capitalism/.

110   Roger Martin. (*The Opposable Mind: Winning Through Integrative Thinking.* (Boston, MA: Harvard Business School Publishing. 2007).

111   The Arbinger Institute. (2016) *The Outward Mindset: Seeing beyond ourselves.* (Oakland, CA: Berrett-Koehler Publishers, Inc.).

112   K. Dancey, C. Tilley, B. Melancon. "The CFO and Finance Function Role in Value Creation." The International Federation of Accountants (2020). https://www.ifac.org/system/files/[ublications/files/The-CFO-and-Finance-Function-Role-in-Value-Creation_0.pdf.

113   B. Roche and J. Jakub. *Completing Capitalism: Heal Business to Heal the*

World, (Oakland, CA: Berrett-Koehler Publishers, Inc. 2017).

114   E. Lawler and C. Worley. *Built to Change: How to Achieve Sustained Organizational Effectiveness.* (San Francisco, CA: Jossey-Bass. 2006).

115   Democracy at Work Institute. "What is a Worker Cooperative." Institute.coop/what-worker-cooperative.

116   BLab. "Certified B Corporation – About B Corps." bcorporation.eu/about-b-corps.

117   Judy Samuelson. *The Six New Rules of Business: Creating Real Value in a Changing World.* (Oakland, CA: Berrett – Koehler Publishers, Inc. 2021).

118   S. Ebrahim, K. Krisnakanthan and S. Thaker. "Agile Compendium." McKinsey & Company (October 2018). Mckinsey.com/~/media/McKinsey/Business%20Functions/Organization/Our%20Insughts/Harnessing%20agile%20compendium/Harness-Agile-compendium-October-2018.ashx.

119   Personal interview by the author with Johannes Dumay, Professor of Accounting, Macquarie University (February 22, 2021).

120   Nassim Nicholas Taleb. (2012) *Antifragile: things that gain from disorder.* (New York, NY: Random House).

121   Ibram X. Kendi. (2019) *How to be an antiracist.* (New York, NY: One World).

122   Kevin Daum. "This Corporate Executive and Non-Profit Director Busts the Myths About Working for Non-Profits." *Inc* (April 12, 2019). https://www.inc.com/kevin-daum/this-corporate-executive-non-profit-director-busts-myths-about-working-for-non-profits.html.

123   Edward T. Hall and Mildred Reed Hall. *Understanding cultural differences. [Germans, French and Americans].* (Boston, MA: Intercultural Press, 1990).

124   William D'Agostino, *This Machine* Copyright (2021). Reproduced in its entirety under license. Inquiries related to *This Machine* should be directed to Juniper Productions, Philadelphia, PA, Attn: Sonya Aronowitz, sonya@juniper.agency.

125   GRI 405: Diversity and Equal Opportunity 2016. https://globalreporting.org/standards.

126   International Standards Organization. *Human resource management – Guidelines for internal and external human capital reporting* (ISO 30414:2018(E)).

127   International Standards Organization. *Human resource management – Guidelines for internal and external human capital reporting* (ISO 30414:2018(E)).

128   International Standards Organization. *Human resource management – Guidelines for internal and external human capital reporting* (ISO 30414:2018(E)).

129   "International Classification of Functioning, Disability and Health." (2001). *World Health Organization.*

130   International Standards Organization. *Human resource management – Guidelines for internal and external human capital reporting* (ISO 30414:2018(E)).

131   International Standards Organization. *Human resource management – Guidelines for internal and external human capital reporting* (ISO 30414:2018(E)).

132   GRI 405: Diversity and Equal Opportunity 2016.

133   International Standards Organization. *Human resource management – Diversity and Inclusion* (ISO 30415:2021(E)).

134   GRI 201: Economic Performance 2016.

135   International Standards Organization. *Human resource management – Diversity and Inclusion* (ISO 30415:2021(E)).

136   "COVID-19 and Child Labour: A time of crisis, a time to act." International Labour Organization and United Nations Children's Fund. (November 2020).

https://www.ilo.org/wcmsp5/groups/public/@ed_norm/@ipec/documents/publication/wcms_747421.pdf

137   GRI 408: Child Labor 2016.

138   GRI 409: Forced or Compulsory Labor 2016.

139   International Standards Organization. *Human resource management – Guidelines for internal and external human capital reporting* (ISO 30414:2018(E)).

140   GRI: 102 General Disclosures 2016.

141   GRI 406: Non-Discrimination 2016.

142   International Standards Organization. *Human resource management – Guidelines for internal and external human capital reporting* (ISO 30414:2018(E)).

143   GRI 407: Freedom of Association and Collective Bargaining 2016.

144   National Labor Relations Act (29 U.S.C. §§ 151–169)

145   "About the Living Wage Calculator," MIT, https://livingwage.mit.edu/pages/about.

146   Coalition for Inclusive Capitalism. "Embankment Project for Inclusive Capitalism Report." (2020).

147   World Economic Forum. "Toward Common Metrics and Consistent Reporting of Sustainable Value Creation." (September 2020). https://www.weforum.org/whitepapers/toward-common-metrics-and-consistent-reporting-of-sustainable-value-creation

148   International Standards Organization. *Human resource management – Guidelines for internal and external human capital reporting* (ISO 30414:2018(E)).

149   International Standards Organization. *Human resource management – Guidelines for internal and external human capital reporting* (ISO 30414:2018(E)).

150   International Standards Organization. *Human resource management – Guidelines for internal and external human capital reporting* (ISO 30414:2018(E)).

151   GRI 403: Occupational Health and Safety 2018.

152   Occupational Safety and Health Administration Regulations (Standards – 29 CFR 1904). *US Department of Labor.*

153   GRI 403: Occupational Health and Safety 2018.

154   Access Economics (2004) "Costs of Workplace Injury and Illness to the Australian Economy: Reviewing the Estimation Methodology and Estimates of the level and distribution of costs." *Reports for the National Occupational Health and Safety Commission* (March 2004).

155   International Standards Organization. *Human resource management – Guidelines for internal and external human capital reporting* (ISO 30414:2018(E)).

156   GRI 403: Occupational Health and Safety 2018.

157   International Standards Organization. *Human resource management – Guidelines for internal and external human capital reporting* (ISO 30414:2018(E)).

158   World Economic Forum. "Toward Common Metrics and Consistent Reporting of Sustainable Value Creation." (September 2020). https://www.weforum.org/whitepapers/toward-common-metrics-and-consistent-reporting-of-sustainable-value-creation.

159   OECD (2019), *Getting Skills Right: Future-Ready Adult Learning Systems*, Getting Skills Right, OECD Publishing, Paris, https://doi.org/10.1787/9789264311756-en.

160   GRI 404: Training and Education 2016.

161   International Standards Organization. *Human resource management – Guidelines for internal and external human capital reporting* (ISO 30414:2018(E)).

162   International Standards Organization. *Human resource management – Guidelines for internal and external human capital reporting* (ISO 30414:2018(E)).

163   International Standards Organization. *Human resource management – Guidelines for internal and external human capital reporting* (ISO 30414:2018(E)).

164   World Economic Forum. "Toward Common Metrics and Consistent Reporting of Sustainable Value Creation." (September 2020). https://www.weforum.org/whitepapers/toward-common-metrics-and-consistent-reporting-of-sustainable-value-creation.

165   WBCSD (2008). "Measuring Impact Framework Methodology." https://www.wbcsd.org/cpntentwbc/download/2208/28100/1.

166   OECD (2019), *Getting Skills Right: Future-Ready Adult Learning Systems*, Getting Skills Right, OECD Publishing, Paris, https://doi.org/10.1787/9789264311756-en.

167   International Standards Organization. *Human resource management – Guidelines for internal and external human capital reporting* (ISO 30414:2018(E)).

168   James D. and Wendy Kayser Kirkpatrick. *Four Levels of Training Evaluation.* (Alexandria,VA: ATD Press, 2016).

169   World Economic Forum. "Toward Common Metrics and Consistent

Reporting of Sustainable Value Creation." (September 2020). https://www.weforum.org/whitepapers/toward-common-metrics-and-consistent-reporting-of-sustainable-value-creation.

170   World Economic Forum. "Toward Common Metrics and Consistent Reporting of Sustainable Value Creation." (September 2020). https://www.weforum.org/whitepapers/toward-common-metrics-and-consistent-reporting-of-sustainable-value-creation.

171   World Economic Forum. "Toward Common Metrics and Consistent Reporting of Sustainable Value Creation." (September 2020). https://www.weforum.org/whitepapers/toward-common-metrics-and-consistent-reporting-of-sustainable-value-creation.

172   World Economic Forum. "Toward Common Metrics and Consistent Reporting of Sustainable Value Creation." (September 2020). https://www.weforum.org/whitepapers/toward-common-metrics-and-consistent-reporting-of-sustainable-value-creation.

173   GRI 401: Training and Education 2016.

174   International Standards Organization. *Human resource management – Guidelines for internal and external human capital reporting* (ISO 30414:2018(E)).

175   GRI 201: Economic Performance 2016.

176   GRI 201: Economic Performance 2016.

177   World Economic Forum. "Toward Common Metrics and Consistent Reporting of Sustainable Value Creation." (September 2020). https://www.weforum.org/whitepapers/toward-common-metrics-and-consistent-reporting-of-sustainable-value-creation.

178   World Economic Forum. "Toward Common Metrics and Consistent Reporting of Sustainable Value Creation." (September 2020). https://www.weforum.org/whitepapers/toward-common-metrics-and-consistent-reporting-of-sustainable-value-creation.

179   World Economic Forum. "Toward Common Metrics and Consistent Reporting of Sustainable Value Creation." (September 2020). https://www.weforum.org/whitepapers/toward-common-metrics-and-consistent-reporting-of-sustainable-value-creation.

180   Coalition for Inclusive Capitalism. "Embankment Project for Inclusive Capitalism Report." (2020).

181   International Standards Organization. *Human resource management – Guidelines for internal and external human capital reporting* (ISO 30414:2018(E)).

182   International Standards Organization. *Human resource management – Guidelines for internal and external human capital reporting* (ISO 30414:2018(E)).

183   International Standards Organization. *Human resource management – Guidelines for internal and external human capital reporting* (ISO 30414:2018(E)).

184   Notice of the Annual Meeting of Shareholders and 2021 Proxy Statement, Prudential. Accessed from https://s22.q4cdn.com/600663696/files/doc_presentations/2021/Prudential-Proxy2021.pdf

185   Notice of the Annual Meeting of Shareholders and 2020 Proxy Statement, Prudential. Accessed from www3.prudential.com/annualreport/report2020/proxy/HTML1/tiles.htm.

186   The Science of Citizenship: 2019 Sustainability Report. Downloaded from https://sustainability.lockheedmartin.com/sustainability/downloads/Lockheed_Martin_Sustainability_Report_Full_2019.pdf.

187   The Science of Citizenship: 2019 Sustainability Report. Downloaded from https://sustainability.lockheedmartin.com/sustainability/downloads/Lockheed_Martin_Sustainability_Report_Full_2019.pdf.

188   The Science of Citizenship: 2019 Sustainability Report. Downloaded from https://sustainability.lockheedmartin.com/sustainability/downloads/Lockheed_Martin_Sustainability_Report_Full_2019.pdf.

189   The Science of Citizenship: 2019 Sustainability Report. Downloaded from https://sustainability.lockheedmartin.com/sustainability/downloads/Lockheed_Martin_Sustainability_Report_Full_2019.pdf.

190   Calculation jointly created by Dave Bookbinder, ASA, CEIV and Laura Kellers Queen, EdD for use in the original presentation of The New ROI Experience (January 2019).

191   Calculations jointly created by Jeff Higgins, CEO, Human Capital Management Institute, Dave Bookbinder, ASA, CEIV and Laura Kellers Queen, EdD for the original presentation of The New ROI Experience (January 2019).